Rx *for Texas*

Rx
for Texas

Staying in Business in the '90s

By David Ronin

Taylor Publishing Company
Dallas, Texas

Designed by David Timmons

Copyright 1989 by Lloyd David Ronin

Published by Taylor Publishing Company
    1550 Mockingbird Lane
    Dallas, Texas 75235

All rights reserved.

No part of this book may be reproduced in any form without written permission from the publisher.

Library of Congress Cataloging-in-Publication Data

Ronin, David.
  RX for Texas: staying in business in the '90s/David Ronin.
  p. cm.
  ISBN 0-87833-689-3: $16.95
  1. Economic forecasting—Texas. 2. Texas—Economic conditions.
I. Title.
HC107.T4R66 1989
338.9764'009'049—dc20
                                                                89-34577
                                                                       CIP

Printed in the United States of America

10 9 8 7 6 5 4 3 2 1

The following publishers have generously given permission to use quotations from copyrighted works: From *The Rise and Decline of Nations*, by Mancur Olson. Copyright © Mancur Olson, 1982. Reprinted by permission of Yale University Press. From *Science and Technology in the World of the Future*, by Arthur B. Brownwell. Copyright © 1970, John Wiley & Sons, Inc. Reprinted by permission of John Wiley & Sons, Inc. From *The Zero-Sum Society* by Lester C. Thurow. Copyright © Lester C. Thurow, 1980 by Basic Books, Inc. Reprinted by permission of Basic Books, Inc. From "Shadow Warriors" by Edward Klein. Copyright © May, 1989, *Manhattan, inc.* Reprinted by permission of *Manhattan, inc.* From an article by Don Sneed. Reprinted by permission of Don Sneed. From *Job Creation in America: How Our Smallest Companies Put the Most People to Work* by David L. Birch. Copyright © 1987 by The Free Press, a Division of Macmillan, Inc. Used by permission of the publisher. From *Cities and the Wealth of Nations* by Jane Jacobs. Copyright © 1985 by Jane Jacobs and Random House. Used by permission from Jane Jacobs. From *The Economy of Cities* by Jane Jacobs. Copyright © 1970 by Jane Jacobs and Random House. Used by permission from Jane Jacobs. From *Bottom-Up Marketing* by Al Ries and Jack Trout. Copyright © 1988 by Al Ries and Jack Trout. Used by permission of McGraw-Hill. Quoted by permission of the publishers from *Dynamic Economics* by Burton H. Klein, Cambridge, Mass.: Harvard University Press, Copyright © 1977 by the President and Fellows of Harvard College. All rights reserved.

Dedication

To Helen Marie and Christopher Lynn, who will reach adulthood in the Texas of the 21st century:

May your future, and that of the Lone Star State, shine brightly and bring much happiness.

Acknowledgements

First, and quite possibly foremost, my thanks to the Houston Public Library, and especially to the people who handle the telephone reference service. Despite budget cutbacks as a result of Houston's economic woes, the staff has remained amazingly courteous and helpful—and, as always, extremely well-informed.

The folks at Rimsco Software, Inc., of Pasadena, Texas, supplied hardware, software, and instruction. Dale, Barbara, and Perri Harper, along with Rimsco associate "King James" Kling, were available nearly twenty-four hours a day, seven days a week — and were badly needed.

On the final draft, deepest thanks also to Chris Niemeyer of the Microcomputer Center and Larry G. Liberty of the Microcomputer Support Group, both at the University of Texas at Austin. These guys saved this computer-illiterate author from a fate worse than death. (See reference to torture, below.)

Several people donated their time to read various drafts of the manuscript for this book, and shared their thoughts about it. Most important of these, in alphabetical order, were: Charmian Akins, former managing editor of the now-defunct *Texas Business* magazine, which would be alive and well today if she'd been its editor in chief; Alan M. Field, a globetrotting financial journalist whose career includes long stints with virtually every major American business magazine; Scott Hakala, an economist at Southern Methodist University, who graciously did not take offense at my criticism of his profession; and Jane Jacobs, one of the heroic figures of "bootstrap economics."

Lee Hoffman, a marketing communications consultant in Dallas, did the best and most thorough editing job this business writer's work has ever received. Although writers and copy editors are natural enemies, she proved that there is indeed at least one exception to the rule.

Stevie Henderson, managing editor for trade books at Taylor Publishing Company in Dallas, championed this manuscript within her firm, shepherded it through several drafts—and held to a minimum the number of cigarette burns she inflicted when I missed deadlines. Stevie's a wonder.

The normal practice is for an author to close the acknowledgements by saying that if there are any shortcomings in his or her book, those to whom the author is indebted are not to be held responsible. Forget that. Whatever is wrong with this book, don't blame me: it's somebody else's fault, not mine, I assure you.

Contents

1   Pollyannas vs. Pragmatists   *1*
Texas as an example • Usefulness for other states • Group-think mentality • Fresh approaches • Changing the economic future

2   Dependence vs. Independence   *6*
Economic alternatives • Historical perspective • "Magic wand" thinking • Facing reality • Potential model for the nation

3   The Longhorns of a Dilemma   *14*
The longhorn of oil • Consequences of vertical integration • The longhorn of water • Effect on agribusiness • Economic impact • Figuring the opportunity cost

4   Extremes vs. Means   *35*
Extremes of economics: Macros and micro • Mesoeconomics as a middle ground • The job-generation process • "Bootstrap economics" as a means to restore an economy

5   Money vs. Wealth   *39*
Difference between concepts • Texas as an economic colony • Tracking the flow of goods • Terms of trade • Sources of inputs • True balance of trade • Value-added as the key

6   Financial Capital vs. Mental Capital   *49*
The ultimate resource • Mental capital adds value • The experience curve • Economic domination • Tacit knowledge • The rewards of development

7   Growth vs. Development   *56*
The Jacobs Model • Development creates new resources • "Tapeworm" economics • Supply regions • Economic engine: exports, imports, economic multiplier, import-replacement multiplier, financial services, value-added, economic infrastructure

8 Import Substitution vs. Import Replacement **69**
Real purpose of imports • Import substitution as protectionist policy • An import-replacement scenario for Texas • The problem with branch plants • In search of the competitive edge

9 Certainty vs. Risk **86**
"Grand" strategy • Media marksmanship • Myths about Japan • "Bottom-up" marketing • Growth paradox • Trade paradox • Technological leadership • Predictable unpredictability • Serendipity factor

10 Industrial Policy vs. Bootstrap Economics **106**
Socialism and industrial policy • Bureaucratic cancer • Rivals enter service industries • Economic Darwinism • Japanese cartels • Assessing methods of increasing employment

11 Entropy vs. Energy **125**
"Ivory tower" planning • Business Expansion and Retention Survey • "Project Team" • Oregon Marketplace • Hidden diversity • A vital distinction • Texas agricultural recovery

12 Texas as a Welfare State **152**
War and the welfare state • Japan as "furnishing merchant" • Industrial strength and military power • Warfare welfare • The return of opportunity cost • Lessons of history • A better role for Texas

13 Texas as a State of Mind **183**
Texas education reform • The media and the message • Asking the "right" questions • Process and product • Employee's new role • Practical payoff • The competition of ideas

14 Starting Over **208**
Banks and capital starvation • Statistics mask deeper truths • Foundation for future prosperity • "Bootstrap economics" as a long-term program • Avoiding the quick fix

1 | Pollyannas vs. Pragmatists

Where seldom is heard a discouraging word,
And the skies are not cloudy all day.
—From "Home on the Range"

When I mentioned to one Yankee that I was working on a book about the future of the Texas economy, he quickly replied, "Must be a pretty short book!" He was right, though not for the reasons he had in mind. (Other jests included speculation that it would be printed in red ink, or that it would start with chapter seven—as in Chapter VII of the federal bankruptcy code.)

However, this isn't a book just for Texas. It also is a case study in "bootstrap economics," with Texas as the example. The lessons it claims to contain would have worked for Michigan or Pennsylvania when those states had big problems, and they could still work for other states in the future. These lessons are drawn not only from economics writers. They also come from the hands-on experiences of economic-development efforts in New Jersey and Oregon, among other places.

For several years, we Texans constantly heard people say, "This is the year we hit bottom. Next year we'll see a recovery." Year after year, the same folks who made that prediction somehow forgot it after their analysis proved inaccurate. However, that didn't stop them from making the same assessment year in and year out.

Now the chorus has changed. Today it goes like this: "Last year we bottomed out. Now a recovery is underway." Maybe so. Then again, maybe no.

One thing is sure: According to the U.S. Small Business Administration, there are two times when a lot of businesses fail.

The first, naturally, is during a depression such as we have had in Texas these past several years. However, the second time businesses are most likely to fail is surprising: It's in the early phase of a recovery.

This is because many businesspeople overreact to the good news of an economic upturn. "Happy days are (almost) here again," they seem to say. Then they go out and spend a lot of money on new assets, to be prepared to take advantage of the impending economic revival.

However, as the old saying goes, "There's many a slip 'twixt cup and lip." Often the economic revival doesn't happen quite as fast as anticipated. Sometimes it doesn't happen at all. Once in a while, the newfound "recovery" suddenly turns out to be no more than a brief and pleasant diversion from a continuing decline.

Regardless of which of these three alternatives occurs, a lot of businesses discover, too late, that their cash flow won't cover their financial commitments. Even though business might be good again, it doesn't become good enough, fast enough. And that brings another wave of bankruptcies.

As a market researcher and business writer, I have interviewed many leaders in government, business, academe, and the media. I've read the published and private reports, and listened to many VIPs at symposia and colloquia.

And there's something odd going on. For several years now, some of our "opinion leaders" have been held in thrall by what's clearly a group-think mentality. This herd instinct is a startling contrast to the pride we Texans have always taken in our rugged individualism.

It's one thing for some politicians and business leaders not to want to be the bearers of bad news, and not to want to bite the bullet. It's quite another for these leaders, especially now, to constantly ignore any and all information that deals with Texas as it really is, not as it once was, or as we'd like it to be. Granted, recently we have seen some positive economic indicators, for a change. But there is still an overwhelming preponderance of bad news. For purposes of morale, it indeed is always better to look on the bright side. But behind the facade of pep talks, we ought to keep a firm grip on reality. There is nothing wrong with well-founded optimism, but there is something very wrong with chronic wishful thinking.

Our economic Pollyannas make much hoopla about one small bit of good news, even when it's taken out of context. This encourages the very sort of idealistic overreaction that the SBA indicates could eventually leave a lot of businesspeople even worse off than they are now.

Those of us who were here before, during, and after the Texas boom recall how the economic reversal of 1982 became an all-out economic bust by 1986. Today, despite the bust, the price of oil easily could fall by another 50 percent. And the U.S. economy itself could go into a major recession, nipping our alleged Texas recovery in a yellow rosebud.

Too many of our leaders don't even want to think about such things, let alone publicly air them. After so many years of dreary news, perhaps we shouldn't blame them. Even so, those who grasp at straws might cause us all to come up empty-handed.

Some people won't exactly welcome this book. In fact, they might accuse it of being counterproductive, as it might cause those in business to hold back on spending and thus delay our purported recovery. Certainly that's what happened during the so-called "Great" Depression.

However, the nature of the American economy then was vastly different from the nature of the Texas economy now. The two situations are comparable only in the most superficial way—but our Pollyannas seem to prefer superficialities.

Regardless of the accuracy of any specific predictions, the Texas situation will improve, eventually. However, when that happens, these same opinion leaders will assert that our troubles are over. But, in a larger sense, our troubles won't really be over even if a full-scale recovery does occur. The mess we're in now was a long time coming. It resulted from attitudes and practices that have been with us throughout Texas history. What happened to us this time around was inevitable, just a question of when. And if we don't correct our basic flaws, sooner or later our economy will collapse again, needlessly.

Therefore, we must take a hard look at what has happened in Texas. That part's easy: The dramatic downturn has been staring us in the face for quite awhile. But it is even more important for us to take a hard look at why this has happened. Most importantly, we need to take a hard look at what we can do about it. Instead of hoping that all will soon be well, Texas needs to start doing the hard-nosed analysis that will keep this from ever happening again.

We need to provide a new foundation for our future prosperity. That's the purpose of this book.

Those who've noted the distress in Texas (whether with pity or pleasure) ought to be reminded of the previous distress in other states. Despite the differences in superficial causes, the ultimate causes were the same elsewhere as in Texas. The effects were certainly the same.

A study of what's happened in Texas, and why, can help prevent economic disasters elsewhere. So while this book is mainly concerned with Texas, it includes material about other states, and about the U.S. economy in general—in part because Texas, at least officially, is one of the United States of America.

Some observers of the economy are predicting a major recession in America soon, perhaps even a second "Great" Depression. Most influential economists deny this possibility. They are the keepers of the conventional wisdom, and have a vested interest in convincing us that Uncle Sam is still fully clothed.

If and when a nationwide recession or depression does occur, these experts will then urge us to turn to the same policies that allegedly worked in the 1930s. Already, some call for another New Deal, in the form of a new Reconstruction Finance Corporation. However, for reasons to be presented in this book, times have changed too much. We can't turn back the clock.

The old answers will no longer work, whether in Texas or in America. Nor will the old questions. Such obsolete approaches cause us to "stumble backward into the future," in the words of Marshall McLuhan. Neither Texas nor America can afford that, because both are stumbling badly now.

Rx for Texas questions the answers provided by the conventional wisdom regarding economic development, and comes up with a different set of answers. It might not give all the answers, or even the right answers. However, at the very least, it might inspire some fresh thinking regarding the future of our economy.

This book has, at times, been written in anger. But it has been a labor of love. It is one individual's effort to challenge the conventional wisdom, and to suggest that the folks on the bandwagon are playing the wrong tune.

2 | Dependence vs. Independence

I met a traveller from an antique land
Who said: "Two vast and trunkless legs of stone
Stand in the desert. Near them, on the sand,
Half-sunk, a shattered visage lies, whose frown,
And wrinkled lip, and sneer of cold command,
Tell that its sculptor well those passions read.

•

'My name is Ozymandias, king of kings:
Look on my works, ye Mighty, and despair!'
Nothing beside remains. Round the decay
Of that colossal wreck, boundless and bare
The lone and level sands stretch far away."

Percy Bysshe Shelley
"Ozymandias" (1817)

ITEM:
White Oak is a town that sits on, and lives off, the fabled East Texas oilfield. More than five billion barrels of black gold have come out of that patch since "Dad" Joiner discovered it in 1930. Now it's running dry.

Oil money, in the form of personal incomes, business profits, and taxes, has built White Oak's homes, churches, stores, and way of life. The town was so dependent on the East Texas field, and so complacent, that it never bothered to develop any economic activity not directly or indirectly connected to oil.

By the end of this century, at the latest, the oil will be gone, and this town—already reduced to 4400 people—will be gone with it. A reporter who interviewed several residents about the situation thought an old domino player (enjoying himself in the oil-financed municipal recreation hall) best summed up their attitude: "We've had our day in the sun. Now we're going to suffer, and there's nothing we can do about it."

ITEM:
Petersburg is a town in the Texas panhandle, about 25 miles north of Lubbock. It has maybe 1600 people. It too sits on, and lives off, a vital underground natural formation. In this case, though, the precious liquid is water, not oil, and the underground formation is called the Ogallala Aquifer. And now the Ogallala Aquifer, like the East Texas oilfield, is running dry. Petersburg—a farming community—is disappearing along with the water.

At one point the community had about forty businesses. More than a dozen of these have closed down in recent years, or have repeatedly changed hands as idealistic new owners tried to flog dead horses. The town had built a medical clinic but was never able to keep a doctor there for long.

It used to have a billiards parlor, which served as the municipal recreation center. The local economy wasn't prosperous enough to support it, though, so the owner sold the pool tables. The place is still open. People play dominoes there now.

The president of the First State Bank in Petersburg told a reporter, "We just tell them [our customers] that something's going to work out in the long run—but we don't know what."

ITEM:
Abilene is the fifteenth largest city in Texas, with about 98,000 people. For years it's lived off the energy industry. But as happened in White Oak, when the energy turned to entropy, the local economy likewise became inert. However, Abilene had the political pull to recover, by means of federal defense dollars. The most spectacular example of this is Dyess Air Force Base, chosen as the home for America's new B-1 bombers. If the bombers ever become fully operational, Dyess will contribute half a billion dollars a year to the city's bank accounts.

Abilene is heavily dependent on Texas Instruments, too, which has a calculator plant there. And General Dynamics, the major producer of war materiel, is also big in the local economy.

So Abilene is completely beholden to outsiders for its economic well-being. Ironically, the townspeople are enthusiastic

8 • RX FOR TEXAS

about their proven inability to pull themselves up by their own bootstraps. A local public relations executive, expressing this misplaced self-congratulation with no trace of embarrassment, told a reporter, "If it weren't for Dyess and Texas Instruments and General Dynamics and Pride Oil, we'd dry up and blow away."

The Texas economy is in deep trouble, and has been for several years now. It seems that the music stopped, and we Texans are the ones left out. As the "Music Man" himself might have put it:

We've got trouble,
Right here in Texas cities.
That's "Trouble" with a capital "T."
That rhymes with "P."
And that stands for . . .
"Petroleum."

The three Items above represent three different responses to our situation:
1. We can sit on our hands, like the old domino player in White Oak.
2. We can turn our hands up with a shrug, like the banker in Petersburg.
3. We can hold our hands out, palms up, and beg outsiders to put money into them—as the Abilene P.R. executive apparently recommends.

But these are not the only possible responses. We also have two other choices:
4. We can fold our hands together, and pray for a miracle. (In fact, rumor has it that several V.I.P. Texas oilmen have secretly converted to Islam. They allegedly get down on their hands and knees five times a day, face Mecca, and pray for a major war in the Near East. They don't care who's involved, or who wins or loses—just so long as it blows the price of oil sky-high.)

5. We can get a firm grip on ourselves, and pull ourselves out of this mess with our own hands—pull ourselves up by our own bootstraps.

This final alternative is the one this book recommends, because it is the only solution that will work in the long run.

We in Texas are in a crisis such as we've never known before. We've had troubled times economically, especially during the Yankee "Reconstruction" that nearly destroyed our economy and did wipe out the state treasury. But the cause of our present crisis isn't political corruption, such as occurred back then. Rather, it's what might be called "intellectual corruption."

In his 1980 book, *The Zero-Sum Society*, Lester Thurow speaks of the American economy. However, his words are particularly apt for Texas today:

> We failed to remember that our supremacy had . . . been based on a rich inheritance of vast mineral, energy, and climatic resources. No one inherited more wealth than we. We are not the poor little boy who worked his way to the top, but the little rich boy who inherited a vast fortune. Perhaps we had now squandered that inheritance. Perhaps we could not survive without it.

Granted, Thurow's statement is an exaggeration. There are many countries even now with the vast natural resources he describes, but which have failed to achieve prosperity, let alone supremacy—economic or otherwise. Still, it's a valid point, especially for Texas.

For nearly 170 years we Texans have looked to the land as the source of our wherewithal. Cotton, cattle, sheep, minerals, timber, and food crops are part of a lengthy list of economic activities that preceded oil and natural gas and the modern agribusiness industry. Historically we've been "Mama's boys," suckling at the breasts of Mother Nature. In this sense, the Texas economy has been living and growing on borrowed time, for a long time.

Thurow is right when he says that America (and, by extension, Texas) is not "the poor little boy who worked his way to the top." But Texas, at least, was a state of very poor boys—and girls—who worked their fingers to the bone, and had little to show for it except bony fingers. Oil changed all that. We suddenly shot from the bottom to the top, just like the Spindletop gusher. But the wheel of fortune has spun again.

We do have one advantage, in that we are still quite willing to work hard. But even this will avail us little unless we also work smart.

Many groups and individuals have been advancing proposals designed to resolve our present difficulties, whether or not a recovery is already underway and destined to continue. This book is one such effort. However, it seems that the others, for all their variety, are based on "magic wand" thinking.

For example, from time to time it's announced that "high technology" is a magic wand we can wave over the Texas economy to instantly solve all our problems. First MCC (the Microelectronics and Computer Technology Corporation), then the Sematech research center—and more recently "Super Clyde" (the superconducting supercollider)—have been touted as our economic salvation. They're helpful and important, to be sure, but they're relatively insignificant in an economy as large as that of Texas.

Overlapping with the quest for high tech is that old Texas favorite: federal largesse. Today, the president of the United States, several cabinet members, two powerful U.S. senators, and several powerful congressional committee heads are Texans. So it's not surprising that our state's leaders constantly go cowboy-hat-in-hand to Uncle Sam. And it's no surprise that Uncle Sam responds—as he has so often in the past. And so today Houston touts the magic wand of "the commercialization of space," and the Dallas/Fort Worth area (as always) relies on contracts for war materiel.

Our approach to Washington has, in fact, been just like our approach to Mother Nature: Repeat our efforts often enough and sooner or later we'll strike it rich; then take the money and run.

Yet, we should have learned by now that the federal government can be just as capricious as Mother Nature. A state whose economy is dependent on government contracts has only one customer. If that customer stops buying, there are no other markets for the wares. Houston's leaders ought to remember what happened when NASA's budget was severely cut several years ago. The leaders of Dallas/Fort Worth ought to remember what happened when the defense budget was severely cut after Vietnam. Instead, so far, the only lesson they seemed to have learned from these experiences is a determination not to let budgets that affect Texas ever get cut again.

Granted, with the array of powerful Texans we still have in Washington now, it's likely to be quite some time before all those budgets are cut. But eventually they will be cut. And when that happens, the effect on Texas will be even more catastrophic—because we will have deliberately made ourselves so dependent on those budgets.

Texas has always had too many eggs in too few baskets—which is why we're a virtual "basket case" now. It's hard to imagine a situation worse than the one we're in. Yet, in *King Lear* Shakespeare wrote, "The worst is not / So long as we can say 'This the worst.'" Perhaps the worst is yet to come. But our economic Pollyannas insist that the worst is already behind us.

The passage from Lear is appropriate, because that character's most famous line is, "I am a man more sinned against than sinning." So today, many Texans still complain that our economic misery is not our fault; it's Arabian petro-politics, or prolonged drought, or an "us against them" mentality in the rest of the country.

However, Shakespeare's readers can see what the playwright's character could not see: Lear's demise was his own fault. So is ours. We built our economy on sand—specifically, oil sands. And, just as King Lear refused to face reality until the bitter end, when it was too late, so we have only recently faced up to our present reality.

We still refuse to realistically consider our future. But for us, unlike Lear, it is not too late.

The history of Texas is a history of confrontations and conflicts. We've challenged Mexico, the Union, Comanches, and Mother Nature. We have won and lost many battles, and a few wars; but we have always endured. Today, the struggle isn't physical, but mental—and we must confront ourselves. To alter a thought from novelist William Faulkner's Nobel Prize acceptance speech: This time we must not merely endure, we must prevail. And we won't prevail if we keep denying the full truth of what it is we're up against.

The ancient Greek myth of Icarus is relevant here—with a modern twist. Icarus put on a set of man-made wings, took off from a tower, and soared. He'd been warned not to fly too close to the sun, though, as the heat would melt the wax on the wings and cause them to disintegrate. Dazzled by flying, Icarus forgot the warning. He soon fell from the sky. Many out-of-state observers now say that the Lone Star State has fallen, a "shooting star" crashed to earth—the very earth from which we pumped so much oil.

The modern twist on this tale is from Malcolm X, the slain civil rights leader. As his version tells it, Icarus survived his plunge, although he was pretty badly shaken up. As Icarus was lying on the ground, nursing his injuries, another Greek happened along who'd observed it all. The passerby began to mock Icarus: "Well, well, I see you crashed."

To this, Malcolm X said Icarus replied, "Yeah, but I was a high-flying S.O.B. while I was up there!"

There's also a deeper moral, namely that because Icarus was still alive, he might eventually be flying high again. The point is, "He who laughs last, laughs best." The fact of the matter is that we Texans were grinning from ear to ear not so very long ago. Now the joke's on us—even though it is a sick joke—and we might as well keep a sense of humor about it.

After all, a lot of the wise-cracking is actually outsiders' expressions of relief that Texans are only human after all, and not the "bionic cowboys" of the modern myth. The "Frost Belt" media created that myth, and we Texans—flattered, for once—eagerly accepted the accolades. (Certain publications and TV networks, which shall remain nameless here, would be quite embarrassed to review the lavish praise they once heaped on the Lone Star State.)

For now, Texas must relinquish its premature aspirations to national economic leadership. But how we handle this crisis, how we handle ourselves in this crisis, and how we handle our critics, will determine whether we can renew those aspirations, eventually.

Were Texas to introduce "bootstrap economics," this state would be a laboratory experiment for the nation. If "bootstrap economics" works here, then Texas could serve as a model for the country.

Texas is down, but not out. Successful economies pull themselves up by their bootstraps, and continue to do so, generation after generation. Those who wear cowboy boots can do likewise. This book shows how.

3 | The Longhorns of a Dilemma

He who would tell the truth must have one foot in the stirrup.
—Arab Proverb

We're quite aware of problems in the energy industry. But the true dimensions of the problem are much larger. We're also aware of problems in agribusiness, but we ignore underlying problems in that industry that are far more significant.

The trauma we've been experiencing in Texas seems to result from problems in these two industries—our two main industries throughout the 20th century. Yet ultimately these are only symptoms of a much more fundamental problem.

Before we can consider ways to improve our situation, we must consider just how bad our situation is now and why it's likely to get worse, despite the talk of a recovery.

The Longhorn of Oil
What's happening now in the oil industry is a repetition, this time on a global scale, of what happened in the domestic oil industry in 1901 and again in 1930.

Prior to the discovery at Spindletop in 1901, Standard Oil had stabilized America's petroleum industry—albeit for the benefit of Standard Oil, and often by unconscionable means. Both supply and demand were regulated through the price mechanism, which in turn was determined by Standard's target return on investment.

Spindletop upset all that by providing a huge new supply of oil. The price per barrel dropped from a dollar, down to three cents! The reduced price meant a potential collapse in the value of Standard's huge investment—and the value of its shareholders' wealth—because the cash flow to recover the investment obviously would be drastically curtailed.

However, Standard soon found that Spindletop was a blessing in disguise. For most other industries, it was a blessing, period.

Before Spindletop, petroleum's main use was for lamps, where it had replaced whale oil. A second use was as a lubricant for wooden moving parts such as wagon wheels; a third, as a softener for leather goods such as harnesses. Its fourth use seems odd today, but back then, petroleum had medicinal purposes. It was directly applied as an ointment for burns, cuts, and sores—petroleum jelly is a legacy of that use. Its fifth use is just plain bizarre: some people even drank it, as though it were mineral oil.

When Spindletop came in, the price of oil fell far below that of coal, on an energy-equivalent basis. Oil then replaced coal as a fuel for railroad engines, for electrical generators, and for steamships. Soon oil was being used to create something called gasoline, and the horsepower of automobiles replaced horsepowered transportation.

The pattern recurred three decades later, in the 1930s. Yet another staggering Texas oil find threatened the value of existing investments by driving the price of oil down—this time to a dime a barrel. The East Texas oilfield very nearly ruined the Texas oil industry. To restore economic order, the Texas Railroad Commission obtained regulatory power. It became the world's new "energy czar," replacing Standard Oil which had been broken up in 1911.

Once again, the glut proved a blessing for the American economy—and a blessing in disguise for Texas. The 1930s and '40s saw the creation of dazzling new products from oil. Today, roughly 2500 products are petroleum-based, from building materials, plastics, fertilizers, and synthetic rubber, to cosmetics and clothing. The most recent is a composite material for aircraft bodies that is five times stronger than steel, yet far lighter in weight. In fact, oil came full circle from its early use as a patent medicine to the wide array of modern medicines and anesthetics now derived from oil.

This most recent glut differs from previous ones in two ways. First, Texas is not the cause of it. Second, the glut has not been a blessing in disguise at all, but a curse—at least for Texas. There have been no stunning new breakthroughs in research that would create a renewed demand for the world's oil. (Standard Oil of Indiana did create some petroleum-based products it called "food," allegedly fit for human consumption. Since these were made from oil, they qualified as "organic"—hence, as "natural foods." Unfortunately for Standard Oil, consumers did not respond positively, even in the heyday of granola.)

During the run-up in the price of oil in the days of OPEC's power, a desperate search for new sources of oil went on around the world. That search was successful. Major new fields are now pumping in the North Sea and Mexico. (The North Slope was discovered before the boom.) Big new finds, as yet untapped, are located in Brazil and Colombia. Several nations not known as large oil producers—such as Angola, mainland China, Egypt, India, Malaysia, Nigeria, and Syria—have nevertheless found ways to substantially increase their production. Other major fields are thought to exist north of Norway and in East Africa.

While all of this exploration was underway, most nations (especially the big importers of oil—other than America) were desperately seeking to improve their energy efficiency. These nations also sought to diversify their energy sources, moving away from oil as much as possible. Their efforts have been so successful that some analysts have predicted that the world's demand for gasoline (which is what half the world's oil is used for) will be 25 percent less in the year 2000 than it was in 1984.

The result of these patterns is that Texas oil is now but a small part of a market where the demand is not growing as fast as the supply. In the face of all this, OPEC probably will not be able to restore a high price for oil. Even if it could, however, Texas would no longer benefit as it did in the glory years of 1973-82.

In the meantime, petrochemical refineries in Texas benefited for a while from the decrease in the price of oil, until the markets for their own products also became glutted. The upper Gulf Coast experienced a construction boom, and industry employment went up again, somewhat. This is good, but not all that significant in the long run.

More significant is that the foreign producers of oil have moved into the "vertical integration" phase. They now make their own gasoline and all the petrochemical products. The new foreign plants have a fourfold advantage, even vis-a-vis the new plants in Texas.

First, they rely on relatively inexpensive feedstocks. Oil from the ground costs much less to get at and bring up in the Near East than does oil in the seabed or in Texas.

Second, the new foreign plants are built at the site of their feedstocks, which saves transportation costs.

Third, they use the very latest technology, which makes them the most efficient producers. The newest plants in Texas can match them, but the old ones cannot.

Last, since many of these facilities are owned by governments, which also own the feedstocks, the resulting vertical integration helps to hold down the price charged to the ultimate consumer.

Saudi Arabia, for example, has established the Saudi Basic Industries Corporation: SABIC, for short. It shares ownership with the major oil companies, which handle most of SABIC's marketing—for now. SABIC can produce its basic feedstocks (ethane and methane) for roughly 85 percent *less* than the average U.S. cost. When Saudi's expansion program reaches its full capacity, it will export the finished products to the United States.

At present, analysts say, it's unlikely that the new competition from foreigners will disrupt *domestic* sales by American producers. In fact, recently the foreign companies have simply been buying out their American competitors. Regardless, the new competition will probably take away the export market of these American plants, whether foreign-owned or not.

In addition, another part of this price restraint is due to the need of various governments to generate foreign-exchange earnings. This gives those governments an incentive to supply the resulting products below cost, if necessary. As Iran and Iraq rebuild their oil industry, the use of government controls to lower the price (while building market share) will increase.

Another reason Texas will never get back to business as usual in the oil industry stems from a fundamental change in the oilfield-equipment industry. This includes manufacturers of pipe and valves and process-control equipment.

Apparently there is no reliable information available on the exact size of the world market for oilfield equipment. But until a few years ago the United States had the lion's share of this market, easily two-thirds. Since Texas evidently had nearly two-thirds of the American share, perhaps as much as one-half of the world's oilfield equipment was made here.

What has occurred in the oil industry itself is now being repeated in the oilfield-equipment industry. During the boom, it was a seller's market; a lot of Texas firms greatly expanded. But the market demand was large enough for newcomers—foreign newcomers. Then the industry went bust, and most of the Texas firms were left high and dry.

However, the foreign firms often were subsidized by their governments. Those firms are still around and, since the subsidies continue, our foreign competitors will be around for a long time to come. Already they have moved in on the American market, somewhat. Before the boom started, foreign competitors held less than 10 percent of the American market for oilfield equipment. But after the oil bust, their share for some items and services has been as high as 70 percent.

This market penetration represents the efforts of firms from dozens of countries, some of which provide a monopolistic market at home, via government edict. And part of this "foreign" competition consists of overseas subsidiaries of American companies. In some cases, these companies began foreign operations to take advantage of a guaranteed market there. In others, the firms sought to employ less-costly workers. Most recently, they've begun operations elsewhere to escape problems with currency fluctuations or U.S. income taxes.

Whatever the reason, Texas is the loser and will remain so. The successful pressure by Texans to lift the embargo on the sale of oilfield equipment to the Soviet Union, our avowed enemy even now despite *glasnost* and *perestroika*, shows just how desperate the situation has become in the Lone Star State. Yet even this is only a delaying action. We will never be able to return to "business as usual" in the oilfield-equipment industry, let alone to the "golden days" of the OPEC boom.

The ultimate reason why is that Texas is running out of oil. Given present rates of extraction, we have only a few years' worth of reserves left. And our present rate of extraction is considerably less than it was ten to twenty years ago. In fact, Texas oil production peaked even before the OPEC boom, in 1972, when 1.3 billion barrels were pumped.

There are those who say there's nothing to worry about. They point out that current oil-recovery technology only manages to retrieve about one-third of what's beneath the surface. The six billion or so barrels labelled "reserves" represent the oil that's sure to be recovered. But, they say, if we could improve our technology and just find a way to extract at least some of that other two-thirds, we'd get a new lease on life. And, if we could somehow get all of the oil that's still in known fields, we'd add 54 billion barrels to our present reserves. Given the current rate of extraction, this would provide another sixty years to solve our problems.

To support this belief, these people cite the development of the acidation process back in 1925. Until that time, the portion of oil recovered was even lower than it is now. But acidation enabled operators to bring played-out wells back into production.

Texas A&M University is hoping to repeat that pattern today with newer (as yet undeveloped) technology. Wayne Crisman, an oilman in Longview, Texas, endowed an Institute for Petroleum Reservoir Management at A&M. And George Mitchell, the Houston oilman, has put his own Houston Area Research Center (HARC) to work on a similar project.

If successful, these programs would accomplish three things: 1) Texas could indeed buy time for finding a way to wean itself from oil; 2) Texas could heighten its position of leadership in oilfield technology; and 3) most important of all, the United States would have more oil reserves, thus boosting our national security.

Experts say there are at least 100 billion more barrels of oil in the ground in Texas, in potential fields. This figure does not include oil that lies under the waters of the Gulf of Mexico in Texas territory. Nor does it include more exotic resources such as shale oil.

The experts are right, but from an economic point of view the figures are irrelevant. For one thing, in the face of decreased consumption and increasing alternatives, it's highly unlikely that the price of oil will ever again sustain a substantial long-term increase. For another, even if a new short-term boom happens, it would eventually become another bust.

Ironically, oldtimers say the boom-and-bust pattern is the surest cause for long-range confidence. They've been through many ups and downs over the years. So they know a rebound is inevitable, though they admit it probably isn't just around the corner.

But times change, and industries change. The boom-and-bust pattern is typical of natural-resource industries. Texas simply is no longer the factor in the industry that it once was. Our oil business is not like the young prizefighter who's won some and lost some and is ready for a new bout in the ring. It's more like a retired world heavyweight champion, well past his prime. Our days as #1 are gone, forever.

The Longhorn of Water
In agribusiness, our attention has been narrowly focused on the chronic problem of low prices for commodities, and on the resulting distress among Texas and other American farmers. Just as we did with oil, we have constantly assumed that everything else in this industry has remained the same, so we concentrate on one item to the exclusion of all others.

As a result, we've been impervious to new developments looming in the background, which are only just beginning to encroach on our attention. Unfortunately, these other matters are so serious that eventually low commodity prices will prove to be the least of our problems.

Back in the 19th century, a lot of Texans found out the hard way that it wasn't prudent to attempt farming west of the 98th meridian. (Austin and Fort Worth are both just inside that line of longitude; San Antonio and Wichita Falls are just beyond it.) It was plain foolish to farm beyond the l00th meridian, the eastern boundary of the Texas "panhandle." The rain simply wasn't there.

But the windmill, and later the internal-combustion-engine pump, changed all that. These allowed farmers (and ranchers) to tap into the Ogallala Aquifer. This is an enormous body of water within the earth, stretching from the Texas High Plains over to eastern New Mexico, and up through the Oklahoma panhandle, eastern Colorado, western Kansas, most of Nebraska (including the town of Ogallala), and on into southeastern Wyoming and South Dakota.

About one-eighth of America's cotton, corn, grain sorghum, and wheat is watered by this aquifer. In Texas, it supplies more than six million acres of crops, and most of the cattle industry. The demand for its water has been so great that in some places the rate of depletion is fifteen to eighteen times the rate at which nature is replenishing it. Even if water use is cut by 20 percent through the adoption of conservation measures, it's estimated that nearly half the land under cultivation will not be able to produce by the year 2000.

Texas agribusiness has tried to make the water go farther, by switching from water-intensive crops such as corn to hardier crops such as grain sorghum and wheat. However, even irrigated fields of these hardier crops produce a much lower yield in market value than does, say, corn. And, with dryland farming, the market value can easily be a mere one-sixth of the yield from water-intensive crops.

Consequently, the decline of the market value of the crops causes a decline in the market value of the land. This means less collateral for a loan. And, if a farming enterprise already has a long-term loan outstanding, such as a mortgage, the drop in market value of the crop means less money available for debt service. In this sense, Texas agribusiness faces much the same problem as the Texas oil producers.

However, the agribusiness situation is even worse, in part because of the oil situation. When farmers cut back on irrigation, they must increase their use of fertilizer and pesticides—derived from oil—to boost the yield. But even though oil prices have fallen from their highs of recent years, they're still much higher than before the OPEC boom. This means higher prices for the fertilizers and pesticides, and higher prices for the gasoline for tractors, combines, and water pumps.

In the short run, the problem seems to concern the relatively low prices for farm commodities these days, and the relatively high prices for gasoline and petrochemicals. In the long run, the same areas in Texas face the ultimate problem of oil: the sources will have dried up.

Back in November 1985, Texas voters approved two measures relating to the state's future water supply. But only $200 million of the $1.5 billion in bonds was designated for projects directly relating to agribusiness. And even those projects involved only the conservation of the existing supply, not the creation of additional supplies. Yet, to repeat, even a 20 percent decrease in water consumption will mean that we lose half the Ogallala acreage by the year 2000.

This is not to argue the case for creating new water supplies for agribusiness. Quite the contrary. There are two reasons why this is not advisable.

The first involves the distinction between water "use" and water "consumption." It takes 184,000 gallons of water to produce a ton of high quality book paper, 30,000 gallons to produce a ton of steel, and 1,000,000 gallons to grow a ton of rice. Even if we take these statistics at face value industry makes much more sense than agribusiness for the future of Texas.

But these figures represent only water "use." The difference between use and consumption is that used water can be treated and recycled; consumed water is, by definition, gone. And Texas agribusiness exhausts 75 percent of the water it gets in any given year. (At that, Texas is still less voracious than the national average of 83 percent.)

This leads to a second reason why the problem of water for agribusiness must be allowed to run its course. The same pattern that's occurring in oil and petrochemicals also is arising in agriculture: an increasing supply of exports in the world, but a decreasing demand for imports.

On the supply side, Third World countries are coming up fast. Both Argentina and Thailand, for example, have boosted their exports considerably. Even though America still accounts for 80 percent of world corn exports, Argentine and Thai exports are nearing the 10 percent mark. Further, Thailand is well-sited to displace U.S. shipments to Japan, Taiwan, and South Korea.

Most countries of the Near East and Africa prefer to import corn in bags rather than loose. But to hold its costs—and prices—down, the United States exports corn unbagged. It begins to look as though we're damned if we do, and damned if we don't.

Many countries, including India and China, have become self-sufficient in food. They don't need anyone's produce anymore. The Common Market countries of Europe have changed from being net importers to net exporters of foodstuffs.

And Saudi Arabia is now a growing factor in agribusiness as well as energy—which makes sense, given its petrochemical connection. A little more than ten years ago, Saudi Arabia produced only 150,000 tons of wheat a year. Now its output is approximately 4,000,000 tons a year. This process is occurring in many lands, with many food crops.

Unfortunately, the relatively few countries that still need the food America can produce often don't have the money to pay for it.

What's even more disturbing, though, is that complaints regarding quality control, which already have plagued America's manufacturing sector, now have spread to agriculture. Many foreign customers have objected to shipments of crops from the United States that are moldy, dirty, or insect-infested. It seems that American (including Texas) farmers have tried to cut costs by cutting the expense of quality control—which seems related to the high cost of oil from which the fungicides and insecticides are made.

This also relates to the high cost of water. Even though the water itself, as with the oil in the ground, is "free," it costs money to get at it and bring it up. There are now more than 75,000 wells in Texas lands above the Ogallala Aquifer. As the water table falls still further, the farmers must drill more wells, and deeper wells, to reach what's left. This brings costs up along with the water. Again, this pattern is almost identical to what the oil industry faces. The crucial difference is that at least the farmers know in advance that the water is where it's supposed to be.

Those who look to expanded agricultural exports as a way to improve the American trade deficit, and the Texas economy, are looking in the wrong place. Back in 1984, for the first time, the combined shipments of all agricultural products by all of America's competitors surpassed the total of U.S. shipments. American agribusiness lost market share in all five of the major export commodities: cotton, rice, wheat, soybeans, and feed grains (including corn). This pattern will continue to worsen.

Texas has not even managed to move in step with the rest of America's farmers on this, even in relative terms. The largest agricultural exports from Texas are cotton and cotton products, along with wheat, animal products, feed grains, and rice. All suffered; some, heavily.

Exports account for only about 15 percent of all receipts for agricultural products in Texas, however. So at first it might seem that the damage was minimal. Yet cotton, wheat, and rice suffered even more with respect to in-state sales. Part of this is due to lower prices for the same quantity of output.

These patterns are likely to remain. As with the oil industry, so with agribusiness: More water, like more oil, would just provide a delaying action, rather than a basic reversal of our ill fortune.

A Waltz Across the Texas Economy

At least one-fourth of the people in Texas, even now, are directly or indirectly dependent on the energy industry. Although agribusiness doesn't directly employ as many people, at least another quarter of all Texans are dependent on agriculture, one way or another. What is less well-known, but even more alarming: The Texas banking system is more heavily dependent on the collateralized assets of, and cash flow from, agribusiness than it is on any other industry, including energy. (Hence the high rate of bank failures in Texas continues, even though the freefall in the price of oil is long since over.)

Texas also has a manufacturing sector. Depending on whose figures are used, somewhere around one-sixth of non-farm employment in Texas is in manufacturing.

That doesn't sound too bad, but the picture changes when we look past the numbers and examine their composition more closely. For one thing, nearly 10 percent of manufacturing employment is—or, was—in oil-related industry. So much for that.

Nearly 60 percent of the total employment in manufacturing consists of people in relatively stable industries, often closely tied to natural resources: lumber and wood products, furniture and fixtures; stone, clay and glass products; primary metals and coal mining; food processing; apparel; and paper, printing, and publishing.

This leaves slightly more than 30 percent of manufacturing jobs in the entire range of non-oil-related fabricated metal products; non-oil-related machinery, electrical and electronic products; transportation equipment; instruments and related items; and miscellany.

This brings us to "high tech," an elusive term too often used loosely and too seldom used strictly. The broadest possible definition would include all the NASA and Medical Center people in Houston, plus the research personnel in the various centers in San Antonio, Houston, and elsewhere, along with the microelectronics manufacturers in Dallas/Fort Worth, Austin, San Antonio, and Houston.

But even if we include service personnel along with those engaged in the production of tangible goods, high-technology employment in Texas is less than 4 percent of the labor force. To put this into proper perspective, the industry would have to continue growing at its present (fairly rapid) rate for the rest of the century, just to equal the present (depressed) level of employment in the energy industry.

There's not much chance of that happening. Projections now call for perhaps 5 percent of all jobs in Texas to be in high tech by then, and the projections may be quite optimistic. But even if they're accurate, Texas will still have fewer people in high tech in the year 2000 than it has now in energy.

Texas clearly held a large advantage over other states in the development of the energy industry; not so, with respect to high technology. Boosters may brag on the fact that the Microelectronics and Computer Technology Corporation (MCC) and the Sematech consortium chose Austin for their sites. To be sure, there is cause for self-congratulation. However, MCC and Sematech are big fish in a very small pond.

The boosters don't mention that Pennsylvania's Ben Franklin Program enabled Carnegie-Mellon University to become the lead institution in winning a $100 million grant for research in applied software. That was one of the most crucial contests in America for the future location of high-technology development—and Texas lost out.

Of the billions handed out by the federal government each year for research in universities, Texas is typically way down the list. In the private sector, California's high-tech start-ups outpace those in Texas each year by a factor of ten. Even Massachusetts is ahead of Texas, and New York and New Jersey aren't far behind. Texas may yet produce a "silicon prairie," but even so it would be a very long time before it would rival Silicon Valley, nor would it solve our woes.

Amazingly, a "boosterism" mentality still prevails in all sincerity among those who should know better. For example, some assert that Texas is much less dependent on the oil business now than it was twenty years ago. Such commentators then present statistics that other sectors of the economy account for a higher percentage of this state's economic activity than ever before; oil has a lower percentage. Therefore, they conclude, the Texas economy is now diversified; the statistics "prove" it.

If someone in a business conglomerate tried this line of reasoning, he or she would be laughed out of the building. If a conglomerate has six divisions, and one of those divisions accounts for 25 percent of sales while the other divisions account for an average of 15 percent each, then the conglomerate is most heavily dependent on the largest division. If the sales of that division fall by 50 percent and all the other divisions' sales remain the same, then sure enough, the largest division no longer is as important and the other divisions are more important than they were.

But the company's total sales have fallen. This means the largest division now contributes 14.3 percent of total sales. The other divisions now each contribute 17.14 percent of total sales. In this way, a corporation can easily "diversify" itself into bankruptcy. Were the situation in Texas not so devastating, this "diversification" argument would read like a "good news, bad news" joke.

Yet, even in relative terms, the diversification argument may well prove a falsehood. This is especially so in Houston, which is still the center of the world oil industry's technology.

As the U.S. oil industry has contracted, many firms have closed their branch offices and moved their most important people in those branches to Houston. It will be a while before the data are conclusive, but it appears that Houston just might be even more dependent on the oil industry now than it was during the OPEC boom.

Another aspect of the boosterism mentality concerns the population forecasts for Texas. Perhaps Texas will have twenty million people by the end of the century. But who will these people be, and what will they be like?

In the decades after the Civil War, Texas had an enormous increase in population, one of the largest in the country in terms of percentage growth. This was a migration of Anglos, mostly from the Old South. They were desperately poor. Even after Reconstruction ended, the growth of population in Texas continued, and accelerated, because although conditions here weren't so good, they were absolutely miserable for most people east of the Sabine River.

Back then, Texas boosters were active, as they are now. Unlike European immigrants who were drawn to the North by tales of cities where the streets were paved with gold, southern farmers were drawn to Texas by dazzling stories of soil so fertile, and rain so abundant, that crops would nearly sow, sprout, and harvest themselves.

When Texas failed to live up to the billing by its promoters, disillusioned farmers turned to radical politics to solve their problems. The Farmers' Alliance, which eventually became what is called the Populist Revolt, was born in Lampasas County, Texas, in the 1880s. As has often been said, revolution is an act of hope.

When the radical politics failed in Texas (as elsewhere), frustrated poor whites took out their anger on blacks.

This brings us to the next great surge of migration into Texas, from south of the border. This occurred during the Mexican Civil War, shortly after the turn of the century. Fortunately for all concerned, this trend coincided with the rise of modern agribusiness in the Rio Grande Valley. The new arrivals were able to find work, and the Texas economy grew. Instead of a vicious circle, there was a virtuous circle—one of economic development. But such is not the case today.

Various observers have long been predicting that Mexico will again plunge into domestic strife on a large scale. Skeptics have noted that this hasn't happened yet, and airily conclude that therefore it never will happen. But if Mexico does erupt, the exodus north will vastly exceed the current migration. And the implications are ominous in both social and economic terms, especially if the patterns of the 19th century should repeat themselves. Even without political upheaval in Mexico, the migration into Texas for economic reasons will continue to increase during the foreseeable future, as the failure of the amnesty program for illegal immigrants shows.

Those who think that population growth in and of itself is a good thing would do well to look at Calcutta, India; Bogota, Colombia; and, certainly, Mexico City.

But our Pollyannas say, "Not to worry." In fact, when the National Planning Association released a report back in 1985 showing that five cities in Texas would be among the top thirty in "job growth" for the rest of the century, many civic officials were delighted, especially those in Houston, which was ranked #1. No one stopped to ask, what kind of jobs?

Fast-food franchises provide jobs. So do janitorial and yard-maintenance services. But how much do these contribute to the overall improvement of the Texas economy? How high a standard of living will the families of these wage-earners have? And what sort of neighborhood environment and educational prospects will these wages allow their earners to provide for their children?

It isn't enough to look just at the quantity of jobs. We also must look at the quality of those jobs.

Most of the hundreds of thousands of jobs that Texans lost during the oil bust were high paying and highly skilled jobs. The workers' incomes were good enough to enable their families to get ahead, not merely to get by. There was enough money to go around so that other families could make a decent living, too. With the bust, all that changed. According to the Bureau of Business Research at the University of Texas at Austin, for every dollar the price of oil fell, the Texas gross economic product fell by three billion dollars.

A 1988 report from the Federal Reserve Bank of Dallas added more bad news: Despite the fact that our Pollyannas say that further declines in the price of oil won't do much harm, the report indicated that for every dollar the price of Texas oil drops in the future, our state will lose another 22,000 jobs. The report was issued in October 1988, when West Texas oil was still $15 a barrel. The price is higher than that now, but it could easily fall lower, much lower.

Out of Sight, Out of Mind—and Out of Luck

What is most often overlooked in the current Texas situation is the "opportunity cost." This is the income that's lost (the cost) as a result of not being able to take advantage of opportunities—in this case, because the opportunities simply don't exist. The opportunity cost of the decline in the state's most important industries is by far the highest loss, even though we can't directly measure it or even see it. However, although it is out of sight, we need to keep it in mind.

Most new firms start by producing for the home market. In the same way, existing firms that add a new product or service usually start by selling to the local market. It takes time to go through the shakedown phase that all new endeavors experience. Even in the best of times, the odds are that out of any ten new companies, three will go out of business within the first three years; four more will be gone within a decade. For new product launches, whether by new firms or old, the failure rate is 90 percent.

When the Texas economy was doing well, the general buoyancy enabled more firms than usual to make it over the rocks that most young companies encounter. A strong Texas economy meant that many companies could find a ready market for their new products, or new firms could break into an established industry and get just enough market share (at the expense of the dominant firms) to survive and begin to grow.

In a dynamic economy, the firms that prevail are usually the innovators, the ones with the highest creativity. In a declining economy, the ones that prevail are those which can 1) draw on the retained earnings they've accumulated over the years and 2) sell off some of the assets they've acquired.

Texas Monthly magazine, for example, was launched just about the time the deregulation of oil prices began in 1972, which boosted the Texas economy. Today, *Texas Monthly* is one of the healthiest and most creative consumer magazines in the country, serving a very "upscale" audience. Yet, with the decline in the Texas economy, advertisers have cut back on their budgets.

This has reduced the magazine's profitability but not threatened its survival: *Texas Monthly* has long since passed through the shakedown phase, and did so during the best possible time. However, even *Texas Monthly* had to solicit an infusion of money from an outside investor, Dow Jones & Company. Had the publication not been relatively strong to start with, no one would have been interested in acquiring a piece of it.

Where *Texas Monthly* succeeded, *Texas Business* magazine failed. It normally takes a few years for a new magazine to reach the breakeven point. *Texas Business* was started three years after *Texas Monthly*. That three-year time difference may have been crucial.

Texas Business had not reached the breakeven point within its first few years, and not even by the time of the oil crunch. Although part of its problem was mismanagement, had the oil boom continued it would almost surely have become profitable eventually. Instead, the magazine was folded.

Other examples of relatively young firms that happened to be in the right place at the right time, and to make the right moves, are Southwest Airlines and Texas International. The former is a robust regional airline. The latter has merged into Continental Airlines, acquired by the parent company, Texas Air. And granted, Continental hasn't been making so many right moves lately.

But in contrast to those two, the biggest single factor in Muse Air's failure (a name later changed to TranStar before its demise) might be a simple case of bad timing: Muse Air tried to take off just as the oil business began its descent. The two crashed together.

In a distinctly different field, the strength of the major metropolitan economies in Texas enabled many arts organizations to thrive, and new ones to form. Most of the larger groups are still doing well enough, but the marginal efforts have all but disappeared. Their luck ran out. And many of the commercial establishments, such as the cafes and restaurants that catered to the patrons of performing-arts houses and to the workers in central business districts, went out of business. The market does not currently exist to justify the risk of starting new activities in these areas. This has a big impact on the quality of life in our cities.

David Birch is a management consultant who holds an adjunct position with the Massachusetts Institute of Technology. He has spent well over a decade studying economic growth and decline. In his 1987 book, *Job Creation in America,* he reported his findings: The key to economic growth is innovation, and innovative companies tend to prefer areas where the quality of life is high.

> High rates of innovation depend primarily on brains, not land or harbors or cheap labor. The key in attracting brains is to offer quality, not cheapness. The successful, innovation-based company will, in general, settle in an environment that bright, creative people find attractive. Otherwise these people won't come.
>
> Cost is no longer an absolute measure; it now is relative to the quality of the people and the environment it provides. A high-cost area that attracts the best and brightest through amenities it offers will, in general, do much better than a low-cost place that offers much less.

Birch's studies indicate that most Texas chambers of commerce are missing the point when they tout the low cost of real estate and office rentals in our major cities, and when they advertise our low wages and relative lack of strong labor unions. They ought to be stressing the high quality of life here.

Even "workaholics" seldom put in more than sixty hours a week on the job. In their time off, they seek social amenities, whether these take the form of natural resources or cultural and sports activities. The chambers of commerce can't do much to salvage the social amenities, especially the informal ones such as an art league or a fashionable night club. Yet the presence or absence of a "quality of life matrix" can have a big effect on a local economy's future development.

Apparently this was the real reason why Midland-Odessa lost out in the competition to become the site of the supercollider. Technically and economically that area was superior to Waco. But the final decision was based on the fact that most scientists and their families would regard Midland-Odessa as a hardship post, whereas Waco is at least relatively close to Dallas and Austin.

The most obvious aspect of the opportunity cost to Texas in the current situation appears in the financial sector. As losses mounted in energy, real estate development, and agribusiness, banks and savings and loans had less money to extend to businesses in other industries. Despite the fact that a lot of oil-related firms are in good shape, most banks will consider energy-related loans only if the borrower can provide virtually 100 percent collateral in non-energy assets.

Here too, fortune favors established companies. Small startup firms don't have the assets to offer as collateral. Their money has to come from investors. Large firms don't necessarily have to borrow from a bank. Instead, they can lay off employees or sell assets to manage their cash-flow situation.

There's another, completely unnecessary, aspect of the opportunity cost: shortsightedness. A good example of this is the prominent banker who went so far as to put a stop to virtually all loans, business or personal, and instead put his institution's money into blue-chip bonds. His investments performed well, and he profited. He felt no obligation to circulate funds in the community that had placed its deposits with him, despite the fact that the money belonged to the people in the community. His explanation was that he did not make loans in industries with which he was not familiar, and all the industries he was familiar with were in bad shape.

Although this banker could have hired the expertise to evaluate opportunities in new industries, he chose to take his depositors' money out of Texas altogether. Even if everyone else went "belly up," he was sure that he would come out all right.

Many private investors have been just as myopic, though less cautious. Witness the huge popularity of Master Limited Partnerships for continued drilling, long after the boom became a bust. Those investors would not consider alternative investments. In fact, some stayed with the MLPs solely to accrue tax-deductible losses, despite the glaring need to make investments for the future of the Texas economy.

If it's losses they were after, the failure rate for new business start-ups, as mentioned, is every bit as good as that for new oil wells. But even a new company that fails leaves behind something in the form of new know-how, if only in the form of knowing how not to do it the next time around. Drilling more wells contributes absolutely nothing to the future potential diversity of the Texas economy.

Compaq—the stunningly successful computer manufacturer headquartered in Houston—was funded entirely by money from New York City and Japan. Houston did gain jobs and revenues from Compaq's success, but not nearly as much as it would have if the capital gains had remained in Texas.

Another opportunity cost is relevant here. The Texas investors who could have at least partially funded Compaq probably still know no more about the computer industry now than they did before. So they most likely will continue to refuse to invest outside of the oil industry or traditional securities such as T-bills and blue-chip bonds.

The decline of even one major industry is thus a "double whammy" against the Texas economy. The first hit is obvious, bringing down a lot of the existing economic activity. The second impact is the delayed hit of the opportunity cost that prevents new businesses from arising to fill the gaps left by the loss of the other businesses.

Even though the purpose of economic activity is to improve the quality of people's lives, the most important asset any economy has is its people. In other words, people themselves are one of the best means to attaining their ends. When an industry falls apart, not only do high-wage people lose their jobs, a lot of high-level skills are wasted.

Most devastating of all, people's lives are destroyed. Entire families are broken up, and the children of those families often have their futures forever blighted by the effects of economic distress. The social aspect of the opportunity cost to Texas is quite possibly the highest cost by far. The rates of alcoholism, drug abuse, domestic violence, child abuse, divorce, crime—all the measures of social disintegration move in tandem with the measures of economic disintegration.

However, assets are inanimate. Dollars don't have souls. An investment gone bad still means money in somebody's pocket. The assets and the dollars get recycled somehow, and usually are no worse for wear.

With people, it's different. When individual lives and entire families are shattered by economic disaster, people don't just go their separate ways. They pay the price, one way or the other, for the rest of their lives. Granted, there are always hardy individuals who almost seem to thrive on adversity, and who always start over. But such people are few and far between, nor does their existence help the battered wife, the abused child, or those who survive the suicide of another.

The worst myopia of all in Texas has been a failure to realize that we should have given top priority to keeping our best "long-term assets" intact; i.e, our people—individuals and families. Instead, we cut social support systems to the bone. Even though we'll never be able to directly measure a cause-and-effect relationship, we will all suffer, in ways small or large, direct or indirect, long after the Texas economy has officially recovered.

Texas is impaled on the longhorns of a dilemma. We'll never recover the "glory days" of our most important industries, which were based on what we extracted from the earth. Yet we cannot allow the present trends to continue, because they'll run the Texas economy into the ground. We must find ways to invest in our own future, here in Texas, to avoid being gored by the longhorns of this dilemma, and to somehow transcend it. That's what this book is about.

4 | Extremes vs. Means

> *To be an economist is, to many people, to be a combination of high priest, guru, and soothsayer; it is to possess a passkey to the secrets of the future.*
>
> —An unidentified economist

In her book, *The Knowledge Elite and the Failure of Prophecy*, Eva Etzione-Halevy relates a wicked joke about three professors stranded on a desert island. They have one can of beans, but nothing with which to open it.

One of the professors is a physicist. He suggests they use his eyeglasses to intensely focus the sun's rays on the top of the can in order to burn a hole in it.

The second professor is a geologist. He wants them to search for a sharp, hard rock with which to punch a hole in the top of the can.

The third professor is an economist. He ponders awhile, then says, "First, let's assume the existence of a can opener."

Such is the nature of economics today, simply out of touch with reality. In his recent book *Profscam: Professors and the Demise of Higher Education* from which the opening quote of this chapter was taken, Charles J. Sykes says:

> The dismal science [has become] a discipline focused on the construction of abstract assumptions rather than ... economic realities.

Conventional economics is divided into two parts, macro and micro. Macroeconomics analyzes data at the highest possible aggregate level—usually an entire nation, sometimes the entire world, occasionally just an entire state. Such phrases as "the 'globalization' of the Texas economy" imply a macroeconomic approach to dealing with our current difficulties. Those who advocate this way of thinking say that we should start by analyzing the world economy, and then should predict the "megatrends" that seem to be emerging. The next step would be for Texas to create a statewide "industrial policy" to bring our economy into synchronization with these alleged world trends.

But what if the "megatrends" are illusory? What if the analytical conclusions are based on erroneous extrapolations of short-run data, or else on generalizations so large as to be meaningless in practical terms?

A big reason we Texans got into trouble in the first place is that the Texas economy has always been "globalized," dependent on the world economy to buy our exports of oil and other commodities. The "megatrends" approach thus seems like that of the crapshooter who, having lost his bet on the first roll of the dice, shifts his next bet to a different number—and doubles up.

The other area of conventional economic theory, microeconomics, is concerned with the individual firm. Its approach is atomistic, hence of limited use in dealing with aggregates at the level of a nation or the world, or even with just a state such as Texas.

Despite the growth of a "cult of entrepreneurship" in recent years, entrepreneurs are few and far between, and most of them fail. Entrepreneurship has a vital role to play in our economy, especially now. However, we won't solve our problems simply by exhorting more people to set up their own businesses.

In terms of the cliche, macroeconomists cannot see the trees for the forest. Microeconomists cannot see the forest for the trees. In the more scientific terms of Gestalt psychology, the macroeconomists are preoccupied with the ground, the economic aggregate; the microeconomists ignore the ground and concentrate on the figure of the individual firm.

Although macro and micro are the two extremes, economics offers no middle ground. Economists must choose the one or the other—and neither is in touch with reality. The unidentified economist whom Sykes quoted in *Profscam* also made this statement:

The trouble with economics is essentially that its practitioners and their theories have been elevated to a status which they cannot justify.

Whether economists have sought this status, or whether it's been foisted onto them, is moot. The fact is that—at least where economic development is concerned—their theories have failed.

Economics is becoming secular theology; the members of the profession, "econo-mystics." Medieval Scholastics debated how many angels could dance on the head of a pin. Modern economists debate the validity of esoteric mathematical models that are out of touch with what's happening in the real world.

In the late 1970s, M.I.T. hired David Birch (introduced in the previous chapter) to do a research project on behalf of the federal government. In 1979, he issued his findings in a report entitled "The Job Generation Process."

Birch called for "an effort to bridge the gap from micro to macro, and having bridged the gap, to begin to understand the job generation process." He also wrote:

> We must understand how the activities of individual firms combine to create aggregate change. For it is individual firms, not some abstraction called "the economy," that generate jobs, export products, utilize natural resources, and through their location decisions, determine the settlement patterns of this country.
>
> We have known very little about how the parts of the economy fit together to create the whole. Our focus has been either on the whole, and the aggregate measure of it (like GNP and its components), or on the individual firm as the unit of analysis, without reference to how firms combine to create the whole.

Over the past quarter century, a number of highly perceptive observers have presented material that now comprises a sufficient body of work to justify a separate heading as *"meso*economics." "Meso-" (pronounced "mez-o") literally means "middle."

Although the term is—perhaps—a new one, the practice of mesoeconomic thinking is not. David Birch is one of its principle creators. Others are Jane Jacobs and Burton H. Klein. Their thinking, supplemented by the macroeconomic work of Mancur Olson, forms the intellectual foundation for this book.

Some of these people apparently are not aware of the work of some of the others. Perhaps they will not appreciate the synthesis in this book, which combines their work. Yet, taken collectively, their efforts may help us avoid the Scylla and Charybdis of macro- and micro-economics that we in Texas (and, for that matter, America) face, as we attempt to chart a course for the future. Texans no longer have that many resources to work with. We had better invest them wisely.

For those who prefer to dispense with the jargon of economic theory, mesoeconomics can also be called "bootstrap economics," for it implies that we indeed can pull ourselves up by our own bootstraps. It starts at a fairly low level of the economy, and then tries to combine the best of the macro and micro extremes while avoiding the worst.

Instead of being forced to choose between the two extremes of conventional economic theory, we need to create a "mean" between them: mesoeconomics. This "mean" is also the *means* to restoring our economy's well-being.

Guest speakers at business gatherings have made it a cliche that the Chinese ideogram for "crisis" (which the Japanese also use in their writing system) is made up of two characters: The first is said to mean "danger," and the second, "opportunity."

The first does indeed mean "danger." However, the second character is not that for "opportunity," but for "loom." This character is in turn partially composed of the character for "thread." The implication is that we can understand the nature of a threat—and the way to overcome the danger—only by grasping the individual threads that have come together to create the situation.

As Confucius himself explained, "Wisdom consists of the ability to separate, and to unite." We must separate the threads from one another, to comprehend them individually. That's microeconomics. At the same time, we must be able to see "the big picture," the total economic tapestry. That's macroeconomics.

Most important of all, though, we must be able to bring the individual strands together and see how they have become interwoven, creating the warp and woof of the overall pattern we observe. That's mesoeconomics. And it's what we need in Texas now.

5 | Money vs. Wealth

The economy of Texas was and is colonial in its basic structure... utterly dependent upon the prices paid in national and world markets for its basic raw materials, whether cotton, cattle, or petroleum.

—T.R. Fehrenbach
Seven Keys to Texas

We've all heard of "rock" music stars who receive millions of dollars from record sales, from concerts and television appearances, and from merchandise sold with their name or picture on it.

Some of these stars assumed the bonanza would continue forever. They spend their income as rapidly as it comes in, instead of investing it in wealth-producing assets that will enable them to live well after the high life comes to an end. They are living from hand to mouth, even though their hands are filled with caviar instead of bread crumbs.

Texas lived like that for years, raking in the money and dealing in millions, mostly without any comprehension that *money is not the same as wealth*. There seems to be a widespread assumption that whenever the price of oil goes up again, things will return to "normal," and we'll get back to business as usual. But as chapter 3 showed, the economic facts don't bear this out.

The key to understanding all this is grasping the distinction between money and wealth. When the price of oil went from $5.25 a barrel under federal price controls in 1971 to its OPEC-induced peak of $35.11 in 1981, this did not mean the Texas economy had become any stronger or more resilient. It simply meant that we had gained an enormous increase in our potential to become stronger and more resilient. And we squandered that potential.

The vital distinction between money and wealth becomes clear in America's trade with Japan. American officials see nothing wrong with sending U.S. grain, timber, cotton, and coal to Japan in exchange for cars, steel, microchips, machine tools, and consumer electronics—as long as there's a trade (i.e., money) balance. And so the American government has been pressuring the Japanese to import more American beef, rice, lumber, and citrus fruits to reduce the U.S. trade deficit with Japan.

(However, then-President Reagan at one point actually asserted that a trade deficit was good for America. This was one of the best illustrations of what presidential candidate George Bush, in 1980, had rightly called "voodoo economics.")

The simplistic trade-balance approach allows—even encourages—Japan to move upscale, technologically. America, by default, goes down. We're becoming a raw materials economy again, as we were 350 years ago.

Many Texans see nothing wrong with this. After all, much of that beef, rice, lumber, and citrus might come from the Lone Star State. But even those Texans who, as Americans, do get upset about Japan, have ignored the fact that Texas has been an economic colony for the rest of America, and the world, for nearly 170 years now.

We have confused the accumulation of money—especially oil money—with the accumulation of wealth. Success in promoting the sale of more Texas beef, rice, lumber, and citrus would only aggravate our condition and further confirm our self-imposed status as a raw-materials economic colony.

The balance of payments (exports minus imports) is normally associated with nations and world trade. We do not think of it in connection with the economies of each of the fifty United States of America, much less with the individual communities within these states. However, no economy, regardless of size, can have a good standard of living if it doesn't import. This is because no community can be efficient and self-sufficient at the same time.

We think of exports and imports as international phenomena only because different countries use different currencies. When making payment for imports, or receiving payment for exports, it's necessary to convert the currencies involved. Thus trade data are collected, really, only to settle up international accounts—

whether deficits or surpluses—with all the nations whose currencies are involved in a given country's international trade.

When it isn't necessary to convert currencies (as with trade between Texas and other states in America, or between, say, Dallas and Houston—all of which are on the dollar), the data aren't collected.

Since the financial arrangements are necessary, authorities also keep track of the flow of goods and services that the monetary data refer to. But to them, this information is apparently of secondary importance. As a result, most observers look only at the money figures that are involved in trade. They're content if those figures show a balance, and rather pleased if they show a surplus. Unfortunately, the statistical "tale" ends up wagging the economic dog.

It's often said that "there are lies, damned lies—and statistics." But the very worst lies are those we tell ourselves, using statistics to tell ourselves only what we want to hear.

Statistics are only numbers. They're supposed to measure reality, but that doesn't mean they always do, or that the particular reality they measure is the one that's most important. We've all heard fine words from public speakers, but that doesn't mean they really understood the situation they were discussing. So it is with fine-looking numbers. All too often we rest content with numbers that seem to contain good news. This has been especially true in Texas.

Far more important than statistics which purport to measure economic activity is the actual flow of the goods and services themselves. This flow is the *exchange of real wealth* among the economies involved in trade.

More jobs, more people, more bank deposits, and rising land values do not necessarily mean an economy is healthy. In the same way, elimination of America's huge balance-of-payments deficits would not necessarily mean that we have reversed our national economic decline. We Texans should know, as many a financial institution has abruptly failed here, shortly after receiving a clean bill of health from its auditors.

A national economy is the sum of its parts. So is a state economy. As long as we insist on thinking of trade only as a transnational event, we miss the crucial point that any trade, even between neighboring cities in the same state, is an exchange of real wealth. And since we look only at money figures—and even then only with respect to international trade—we fail to note the most important activity: the on-going process of wealth-creation (or wealth destruction) that's involved in any trade, whether between cities within a state, between states, or between nations.

The content of the trading shows the difference between gaining and losing real wealth, as opposed to gaining or losing money. Again, trade between the United States and Japan offers the clearest illustration of this. But at least in this case we do keep track of the composition of the trade, as well as the money data.

Unfortunately, individual states or cities don't have access to such data regarding their own economies. As a result, they don't have feedback as to the health of their economies in real terms. So they don't know what's actually happening in terms of gain or loss in net wealth—until it's virtually too late to change the situation.

The economic crisis that Texas is still in right now is not so much the result of the drop in prices for agribusiness commodities and oil, as it is the result of our longstanding confusion of money with wealth.

Despite the financial data involved, trade is ultimately a matter of barter. Even though financial data are kept only with respect to international trade, the same barter process exists with respect to the economic life of every community, and every state.

"Terms of trade" is the starting point for describing this. The table shows various possible terms of trade. This indicates how much wealth produced in Texas must be exchanged with other economies, using two imported items as examples.

But the terms of trade hardly begin to tell the real story, for they ignore the true costs of producing the Texas wealth that is used in trade. To understand how much wealth we must really create to import a $15,000 car or a $500 stereo, we need to look at where the inputs come from that are used to produce that wealth.

Especially in the case of agribusiness, it's apparent that, in terms of dollar value, most of the inputs come from outside the Texas economy. This means that Texans must create that much additional wealth for export, just to be able to acquire the inputs that in turn create those exports that eventually contribute to a

Terms of Trade
Selected Texas Commodities

Texas Cotton

Price Per Pound	Exports Required to Import a $15,000 Car from Detroit	Exports Required to Import a $500 Stereo from Boston
25 cents	approx. 125.0 bales	approx. 4.2 bales
35 cents	approx. 89.3 bales	approx. 3.0 bales
45 cents	approx. 69.4 bales	approx. 2.3 bales
55 cents	approx. 56.8 bales	approx. 1.9 bales
65 cents	approx. 48.1 bales	approx. 1.6 bales
75 cents	approx. 41.7 bales	approx. 1.4 bales

Texas Cattle

(Based on 1100 pounds per head, on the hoof, of fatted cattle)

Price Per Hundred-Weight	Exports Required to Import a $15,000 Car from Detroit	Exports Required to Import a $500 Stereo from Boston
60 dollars	approx. 23 head	approx. ¾ head
65 dollars	approx. 21 head	approx. .70 head
70 dollars	approx. 19 head	approx. ⅔ head

Texas Oil

Price Per Barrel	Exports Required to Import a $15,000 Car from Detroit	Exports Required to Import a $500 Stereo from Boston
10 dollars	1500 barrels	50 barrels
15 dollars	1000 barrels	33 barrels
20 dollars	750 barrels	25 barrels
25 dollars	600 barrels	20 barrels
30 dollars	500 barrels	17 barrels
35 dollars	429 barrels	14 barrels

higher standard of living for Texans.

Worse, conventional economic wisdom ignores the fact that, regardless of the terms of trade, exports are sacrifices on the part of the local economy. If we think of an economy as a collection of individuals, then this point becomes clear. An economy makes sacrifices just as an individual does, in order to receive income from the "outside."

From the individual's perspective, the most obvious sacrifice is time. We give up a significant percentage of our lives to get the income for our livelihood. Since most jobs involve sacrificing at least forty hours a week of our time, the obvious goal is to get as high a return as possible.

Yet an individual sacrifices much more than time. There's also the money to be spent on transportation to and from work, on clothing that's appropriate for the workplace, and on the training or formal education to qualify for the job in the first place. These are all additional inputs we must pay for in order to gain income. And, if we've borrowed any of the money that pays for these inputs, the debt service can considerably reduce what we have left at the end of each month.

So it is with an entire economy. What's left in the local economy after importing the necessary inputs gives us a clearer picture of the true balance of trade. It makes all the difference in the world whether exports are being used to buy imports that merely enable us to "hold our own," or to purchase those imports which enable us to get ahead and live "the good life."

But there's a vital distinction between an individual and an entire economy. If a given economy can begin producing, itself, more of the inputs that are used in the creation of wealth, it can dispense with those imports that were used as inputs before. When it replaces those imports with internal production, it avoids the sacrifices involved in producing wealth to be exported in exchange for necessary imports. Further, the new local production by itself makes the local economy larger, healthier, and more vigorous.

An individual who tries to increase his or her wealth by, say, walking to work to save money, or by trying to make his or her own clothes, usually ends up losing more than is saved. But because an economy has many individuals and firms, each of which can specialize in a particular type of production, the more self-sufficient a particular economy becomes, the better off it is. This brings us to the concept called "value added."

"Value added" is what an economy (or just a firm, for that matter) provides in the process of transforming inputs it acquires from the outside world. It's a basic concept, one that business people and economists are very familiar with. But it seems that familiarity has bred contempt, at least in Texas.

For example, Texas ships its onions out of state, to places such as Chicago, where the onions are sliced, breaded, and packaged, then shipped back to Texas for sale in local stores. If the typical food-industry percentages apply, 40.1 cents of each dollar of the retail price goes to the processing and packaging in Chicago; 5.3 cents pays for transportation out of and back into Texas; 20.3 cents goes for advertising and other costs, some of which may stay in Texas; and the retailer gets only 3.8 cents, leaving 30.5 cents for the farmer. And most of that 30.5 cents probably leaves Texas to pay for more imports to grow more onions.

Another example: Anderson Clayton, once a Houston-based independent multinational corporation, used to buy so much vegetable oil each year that it took the equivalent of all the soybeans grown in Texas to produce it. But were any of those soybeans turned into vegetable oil in Texas? No. That was done in Kansas and Arkansas, where Texans shipped their crop for processing.

Despite the added costs of transportation, it was still less expensive for Anderson Clayton to do business with the people of Kansas and Arkansas. The people in those states were more efficient at processing soybeans than the people of Texas were. The economies of Kansas and Arkansas got to keep the value added, which means the standard of living of their people, not our people, got a boost.

The main products of colonial economies, such as Texas, are raw materials and basic components. Advanced economies then buy these inputs and apply highly skilled labor, using complex machinery relying on engineering and management expertise. Such economies then sell the raw materials and components back to the colonies in the form of highly sophisticated manufactured goods, such as cars and compact disc players.

The missing ingredient in these colonial economies is that they never invested in themselves. Advertising has confused the distinction between spending and investing, by urging us to "invest" in everything from diamond jewelry to a vacation in Jamaica. But a real investment is a financial sacrifice for something that will (or should) someday generate financial rewards to the investor.

An economy that's investing in itself, not just in assets to help generate exports, is gradually building up the potential for economic independence. In the same way, an individual who builds up personal wealth can become independent of the need to sell his or her skills to an employer.

This does not mean that an economy isolates itself from the outside world, any more than a wealthy individual isolates himself or herself from the outside world (notwithstanding Howard Hughes to the contrary). What it does mean is that the local economy, like the wealthy individual, has greater control over its own future, and is not at the mercy of the outside world. Texans have been at the mercy of the outside world all along. But it's only now that our helplessness has become so glaringly apparent.

Now, consider California. Although most Texans would like to dismiss California as the "granola state" (all flakes, fruits, and nuts), the sad, simple fact is that our fellow Sun Belt residents to the west have consistently outperformed us. Worse yet, the gap is widening, and likely to continue widening at an increasing pace.

Today, even though California's population is only 1.6 times that of Texas, its aggregate personal income is nearly twice as high. Yet California's bank deposits are less than 1.5 times our volume. In short, Californians work smarter than Texans, and they make sure that their dollars work a whole lot smarter than ours do.

In many ways, though, the California economy is similar to that of Texas. California, like Texas, started as a raw-materials colonial economy, although its main commodity was gold, not cotton. Both states later shifted to oil as their principal product. In fact, until 1928, California yielded more oil each year than Texas.

Today, both California and Texas are in the highest ranks for cotton production, shipments of finished Portland cement, and cash receipts from all farm commodities and livestock, year after year.

California and Texas are also the top states in the nation for building construction and retail sales each year. And oil is still big in California: The state is the fourth-largest annual producer after Texas, Alaska, and Louisiana.

So a lot of colonial-type industries are still well-represented in California's economy. And there's no reason why they shouldn't continue to hold a prominent place in both California and Texas. However, the difference is that, for California, the natural-resource industries were just the starting point for economic development. For Texas, they have nearly meant the end of prosperity; ironically, because of our dependence on the outside world.

There's an even bigger reason why we made a large mistake in not moving away from our excessive reliance on extracting raw materials: We are exhausting the natural resources of this state. Ultimately, this exhaustion of our natural resources is the single most important element of our trade. But it never shows up in the statistics of Texas exports, per capita income, or other economic reports.

Chapter 3 described the depletion of the Ogallala Aquifer, mainly with regard to farming. But 40 percent of America's beef supply is raised on land over the Ogallala Aquifer. And the cattle industry consumes water on an even larger—and less efficient-scale than farming: It takes 4,000 gallons of water to raise one pound of beef. Again, that's water consumption, not use. That water is gone; it cannot be recycled, because it no longer exists.

The depletion of our oil reserves needs no further comment.

This exhaustion of our natural resources is the ultimate sacrifice involved in exporting from Texas. What do we have to show for it, in assets that can continue to produce wealth in the future?

The presence of a lot of money does not determine the health of an economy. It's the other way around. The cart, and the load, must follow the horse. As long as money represents the potential to create new wealth, and to claim a share of it, money and wealth are virtually identical.

But when an economy declines and loses its ability to provide for its future economic security, money loses its value within that economy. The extreme example of this is Weimar Germany in the 1920s. There people literally traded wheelbarrows filled with currency, paper money with a face value of millions of dollars, for even a tiny amount of food or gasoline.

Now that Texas is losing its natural-resource wealth as the basis for its future income, what do we as Texans have to offer in exchange with the other economies of the world?

6 | Financial Capital vs. Mental Capital

It is the genius of a people that determines how much oil shall be reduced to possession. The presence of oil in the earth is not enough.

Gold is where you find it, according to an old adage. But judging from the record of our experience, oil must be sought first of all in our own minds. Where oil really is then, in the final analysis, is in our own heads.

—Wallace E. Pratt (1885-1981)
Petroleum Geologist and Executive
Humble Oil Company

The prime source of value added is capital: financial capital, but even more so, mental capital. Engineering and managerial skills, and scientific research, are good examples. Highly skilled manual labor also represents investment in mental capital by the workers who have acquired the skills. And, in fact, the equipment the workers use is a manifestation of mental capital.

Natural-resource industries, on which the Texas economy is still based, provide fairly limited scope for the application of advanced skills. With the exception of petroleum technologies, they do not offer much chance to accumulate mental capital.

The very word "capital" comes from the Latin caput/capitis, which literally means "head." In the words of economist Julian Simon, the human mind is the "ultimate resource." It does not deplete, although it is definitely irreplaceable. And it's renewable; in fact, it must be renewed, in a competitive economy. Best of all, the more we use it, the more we have of it.

There's mental capital in the natural resource industries, to be sure. However, the effort is directed against nature and its capriciousness: failed crops, floods, hoof-and-mouth disease, dry holes, drought, and fish that aren't where they're supposed to be found.

It's a different story with the high value added industries, such as manufacturing. There the mental capital ultimately involves a struggle of each individual against himself or herself. It's a struggle to push one's know-how into new frontiers. It's also a struggle of individuals and groups competing against one other.

If all we're doing is growing produce and selling it, growing cotton and selling it, cutting timber and selling it, raising cattle and selling it, or pumping oil and selling it, we aren't adding much value. Value added occurs only when the crops get processed and packaged, the timber is crafted into furniture and houses, the cattle are turned into beef and leather products, and the oil becomes fuel or petrochemicals. Even so, in each of these cases the finished product is recognizable as a transformation of something existing in nature.

Contrast these items with a semiconductor chip, a compact disc, a jet airframe—all of which are among California's prime products. In each case, the physical item is a manifestation of the bounty of the human mind rather than of Mother Nature. These products are so advanced, so creative, it's as though human beings have fashioned something out of nothing—which, in a sense, they have.

Mental capital is the only source of innovation. And it is only through innovation that we can overcome the disruptions caused by falling commodity prices or the loss of markets—any markets, whether for raw materials, basic components, or advanced equipment.

In the mid-19th century, Japan consistently ran a large trade deficit (those were the days!). Its principal exports were tea and raw silk; not much value added there. When the British developed tea plantations in India, the Japanese lost out against the new competition. But Japan improved the quality of its woven silk and began manufacturing fabric. Japan then replaced its raw-material exports with fabric exports and so helped make up for the loss.

This pattern has been constantly repeated in Japanese economic history. Today, as Korea and Brazil begin to encroach on Japan's export markets for automobiles and steel, the Japanese are moving into industries (including services) that require mental capital on the cutting edge of technology. This is why Japan, with so few natural resources, has consistently been able to increase its real wealth. The postwar Japanese "economic miracle" simply restored an old pattern of economic development in Japan.

The driving force behind innovation is competition. Normally, economics talks in terms of supply and demand. When a supplier cuts the price, the demand is supposed to go up. This doesn't work as well with commodities, though, because most markets for commodities are already stabilized as to their needs. However, an exception is when a new market is discovered through innovation, as happened when oil became the fuel for steam engines and automobiles as a result of its staggering drop in price after Spindletop.

With manufactured goods, the law of supply and demand tends to work quite well. We've all heard of "economies of scale." The more items produced at any one time, the less it costs per unit to produce them. However, economies of scale is a static concept, in that it applies to production at any given moment in time.

In a dynamic, expanding industry, the relevant concept is the "experience curve," a variation on the learning curve. The Boston Consulting Group refined the concept of the learning curve, applied it to manufacturing, and renamed it.

The experience curve includes economies of scale, in that the cost of the fixed investment (factory and equipment) gets spread out over more and more items over time. But the experience curve takes mental capital into account. The more experience a manufacturer builds up, the more know-how the firm's managers and employees gain. They find ways to increase output from a given amount of inputs, or to cut the amount of inputs required for a given amount of outputs. They work the "bugs" out of the system. (To some extent, this happens in commodity production too, but the limits of productivity tend to be reached pretty quickly.)

Because costs drop, the firm can drop its prices, too. This is the typical pattern in a growth industry, such as semiconductors. Unlike commodities, however, a reduction in price boosts the demand for the product. And even though the revenue per unit is lower, the total revenue is higher than before because of the increased volume of sales. Furthermore, the increase in output allows costs to continue to drop. This is the experience curve at work. Competing firms will further reduce prices in order to gain a larger market share and gain still more benefits from the curve.

Eventually a cost "floor" is reached, of course. This is a sure sign that a given technology has matured, or that a given industry has stagnated. The American automobile and steel industries illustrate the latter, although they claim to illustrate the former. They chose to rest on their laurels rather than go for productivity improvements based on new technologies developed by foreign rivals. The Japanese reaped the benefit of the folly which these firms sowed.

In a manufacturing industry, the cost floor can be staggeringly lower than the initial cost of production. This tends not to be the case in natural-resource industries. The productivity improvement is what mental capital is all about. It results from experience, on the job. It isn't something that exists in an ivory tower or a research institute isolated from the realities of production. If such were the case, the Europeans would never have lost their technological leadership to America.

This mental capital is almost a nebulous thing, something like atoms in the physicist's cloud chamber: We can't directly see atoms, or even photograph them, but we can see the tracks they leave behind as they pass through the clouds in the chamber. We have to observe mental capital indirectly, too, by measuring the value added it leaves behind as it moves through the economy.

Brainpower by itself isn't enough to add value. It isn't merely a matter of advanced degrees in high technology, or of research and published papers, even though these can help, a lot. Mental capital isn't even a matter of creating prototypes and first-stage production. Mental capital is a matter of efficient, innovative production for the market: brainpower in action; working smarter; yielding measurable, marketable wealth for the economy. Mental capital is the crucial element for producing goods and services that win out in the competition of the marketplace, because they are superior in quantity or quality in return for the buyer's money; i.e., value added.

We can't *buy* mental capital in the way that we can endow professorships in science at the University of Texas or at Texas A&M, and then raid the faculties of the top schools on the east and west coasts. Nor can we just educate students in technological disciplines, place them in high-tech firms, and assume that this alone will ensure our future well-being. It doesn't work that way.

Mental capital is the union of theoretical knowledge and practical experimentation while pursuing success in the marketplace. It is conceived in scientific research and mental abstraction, and born in its practical applications. However, it can be stillborn—as happened so often with European technology that was successfully manufactured only in America, and now with American technology that's being successfully manufactured only in Japan.

Scientist Michael Polanyi coined the term "tacit knowledge" to describe the know-how that's acquired from experience. As boys and girls, we didn't gain much useful knowledge of the opposite sex from reading books, and not all that much from watching movies and television. Yet by the time we came of age, we'd acquired a vast knowledge as a result of moral teachings and sex education, whether formal or informal. This told us the way things are, or should be, between men and women.

What counts, though, is the way we apply those lessons in practical experience—and in the process we learn a lot of things no instruction (formal or informal) could provide.

For the individual who has no intention of starting a family, this "tacit knowledge" can suffice for a lifetime of interaction with the opposite sex. But from society's perspective, the purpose of gaining the tacit knowledge is to make a wise choice of a lifetime partner with whom to procreate. Despite the romantic notions attached to love and marriage, the underlying purpose of matrimony is to produce children who will have the benefit of a strong and stable home environment.

Thus, marriage is the culmination of prior knowledge, children the innovation for new knowledge—although marriage, in itself, provides a lot of new knowledge for the partners. Responsible adults are the results of society's past successes. Children well-cared-for are society's hope for future successes.

Just as no society will survive if it does not somehow provide potential future members of that society, so no economy is likely to survive if it does not provide future potential members (firms and technologies) for its sub-system within society. And just as the tacit knowledge of the relationship between men and women is the best means of providing a viable innovation—children who will grow up to become a credit to their parents—so the tacit knowledge in the form of mental capital is the best means of providing viable, home-grown technologies and industries.

Texas historian T.R. Fehrenbach repeatedly stresses a point in his works:

> A superior culture—superior in the realities of organization and power—always has attempted, and always will attempt, domination of other cultures upon which it impinges. The means can be in question; the practice, never.

The best-known and most brutal means by which a superior culture dominates an inferior one is war. But economic domination is far more efficient, and it's certainly more beneficial to the superior culture. The British knew this all along; the Japanese learned it the hard way but now prove that they learned the lesson well.

What Fehrenbach calls "the realities of organization and power" are the source of real wealth. And real wealth consists of productive capacity, which in turn is the result of mental capital.

Real economic health is comparable to good nutrition. Both "junk foods" and real foods provide calories. In fact, most junk foods provide a lot more calories than real foods—and calories provide energy for work. However, in the long run a healthy metabolism depends on numerous biochemical processes that are often quite subtle, complex, and seemingly minor. If one key ingredient is missing from the diet of a human body, that body will eventually die, no matter how many calories it takes in, even if that nutrient is required in amounts so small as to seem hardly worth the bother.

Not so long ago, many Texans were tenant farmers. Their diet consisted of cornbread and cane syrup. Pellagra was the result. Today, Texas as a whole has a bad case of economic pellagra. But some are unwilling to face that fact, even now, or to diagnose its true cause. Others are recommending cures worse than the disease itself.

In an advanced economy, with a lot of mental capital and high value-added industries, money is the means by which the economy facilitates the creation of completely new wealth, as yet unknown. The advanced economy is future-oriented instead of backward-oriented. Its mental capital and value-added industries function almost like an insurance policy against economic disaster.

In this case, money is the means to claim people's energies: potential energy in the form of mental capital, and kinetic energy in the form of physical labor. Money becomes the factor that enables people to quickly organize themselves, and their existing material goods, into activities that will create a higher standard of living. Mental capital is what gives money its value.

A Sufi proverb says, "He who would seek the wealth of the Indies must carry the wealth of the Indies with him." This is where we in Texas make our biggest mistake. The real strength and resilience of an economy is its people, not its natural resources or its money. If we will devote more attention to developing the "ultimate resource" of our minds instead of the natural resources of the earth—if we will rely more on what comes out of our heads than what comes out of the ground—then we will yet have greater wealth than the oil patch ever produced.

7 | Growth vs. Development

It is well and good to conserve and to effectively and efficiently use the resources we now have, but if we are to regain what we've lost, we must produce new resources... Our present standard of living is based on past decisions. We must have new resources just to keep pace with our existing commitments.

—Dr. George Kozmetsky
Director, IC2 Institute,
University of Texas;
Co-founder of Teledyne, Inc.

We in Texas not only confuse money with wealth, we confuse mere growth with real development. The difference between the two is crucial. An economy can grow quite large, in terms of money, without developing itself much, in real terms, at all. Growth without development means merely replicating existing economic resources. Development, in contrast, means creating new resources that gradually become independent of the dominant industries of the status quo.

To appreciate the difference between growth and development, contrast a tapeworm with a fertilized human egg. Both exist within the body of the human host. Both feed on nutrients in that body. And more than one of each can exist within the host simultaneously.

But, as a tapeworm grows, it just gets bigger; it doesn't really change. The fertilized human egg, though, rapidly becomes a complex organism, passing through many distinct phases—so many that biologists give each phase its own name (blastomere, morula, blastula, gastrula, etc.). And if all goes well, the fertilized human egg eventually will be able to literally stand on its own two feet.

As chapter 5 noted, an economy must export to survive. Also, the higher an economy's value-added, the higher its potential standard of living. Unfortunately, while both exports and value-added are necessary for genuine economic development, they aren't sufficient by themselves. If the host society depends only on these two, the city, state, or nation is practicing "tapeworm economics" instead of functioning as an economic embryo.

A good example of "tapeworm economics" is Michigan. Michigan is virtually a one-industry state; i.e, automobiles. When imported cars reduced the sales of American-made cars, Michigan had a recession. The state's leaders sought protection from Uncle Sam. And they got it, in the form of the so-called Voluntary Restraint Agreement with you-know-who.

But Michigan's leaders then foolishly assumed that their problems were solved. As the state's economy recovered, they failed to see the protection as offering only a "breathing spell." Instead, they immediately went back to business as usual: more of the same. They deliberately refused to use the protectionism as an opportunity to create new resources that would be independent of the need for political favoritism. Michigan's leaders were too proud, and too complacent, to admit that their state was badly in need of economic development. Michigan remained a one-industry state, foolishly content that "happy days" had returned.

As usual, Detroit's auto executives badly underestimated their competition. In hindsight, the foreign manufacturers' response was virtually predictable. They had too large a share of the American market to simply give in without a fight. They responded by constructing factories in the United States. And so, once again, "foreign" cars—but this time made in America—are causing problems in Michigan's economy. But now no "quick fix" is in sight.

To be sure, Michigan's economy is quite large, with a high level of both exports and value-added. Since these usually result from mental capital, it's worth a brief review of the brainpower at work in the auto industry.

Automotive engineers and executives come to mind first. Then there's the capital represented by the sophisticated machinery the workers use. As for the mental capital of skilled labor: Some of the most highly skilled blue collar workers in the entire world are the tool and die makers of Detroit. In fact, they're part of the "aristocracy" of industrial labor.

Yet Michigan continues its earlier mistake of too much specialization. Even so, this is only one aspect of its problem, because lots of exports from diversified industries will not, by themselves, mean that an economy is truly developed.

Economic diversity is necessary but, as with exports and value-added, this still isn't sufficient. If an economy's activity is dominated by exports—regardless of the value-added or the diversity of those exports—then it is still specializing: specializing in exports. It is still dependent on the outside world. Its activities involve money, in the form of cash flowing in, but there is little creation of wealth.

Jane Jacobs has coined the term "supply region" to help explain this problem. And her description, in *Cities and the Wealth of Nations*, fits Texas to a "T":

> Rich or poor, supply regions are inherently overspecialized and wildly unbalanced economies, hence unresilient and fragile, helpless when they lose their fragments of distant markets ... The reason such regions are specialized and narrow is that, in the first place, their production for others so overwhelmingly outweighs production for themselves.

Her description also fits Michigan—even more obviously than it does Texas. Each year, Michigan's economy produces millions of cars for export to other economies. So the standard of living in Michigan depends overwhelmingly on the willingness and ability of other economies, mostly other local economies in America, to absorb all that production. The people in Michigan are puppets—not of auto executives and labor officials, but of ordinary people outside Michigan.

Consequently, when ordinary people outside of Michigan decided to start buying foreign cars, the people of Michigan had a big problem. One irony of this is that the Japanese, Koreans, and Germans have simply done to Detroit what Detroit did to France and England at the turn of the century. But, in each case, the victims have no one to blame but themselves.

This is not to argue that it was a mistake for the U.S. auto industry to be concentrated in Michigan. Rather, the mistake was in allowing the Michigan economy to become overwhelming dependent on the U.S. auto industry. There's a big difference between the one and the other.

If that industry had been just part of Michigan's total economic activity, then the loss of auto markets to foreign competition would not have had such a devastating impact on the overall Michigan economy. There would have been plenty of opportunities in other lines of work, and plenty of people around who already had know-how in those businesses and could quickly train the newcomers.

Instead, Michigan's people were like those who are on mood-control drugs. When the pills ran out, and the people of Michigan suddenly had to go "cold turkey," they couldn't cope.

In the same way, the people of Texas have also been dependent, mere serfs in a colonial economy of our own making. The fact that some of our puppets have (or had) a net worth of a billion dollars or more merely serves to disguise the fact of their utter dependency—despite the fact that the disguise appears to work pretty well for much of the time.

Once we distinguish between mere growth and real development, we can focus in more closely on the various aspects of economic development.

A highly successful economy is as complicated as a human embryo. However, in deference to the long-standing, mutually beneficial relationship between the dominant industries of Michigan and Texas, let us instead compare an economy to an automobile engine.

A successful economy, like an engine, is based on the dynamic of what Jane Jacobs calls a "reciprocating system": Each part not only contributes to overall economic performance, but contributes to the performance of each of the other parts as well. The system is symbiotic in operation, synergistic in effect. When everything is properly synchronized, the well-tuned economy can go from zero to sixty in a matter of seconds, figuratively speaking.

The Battery: Exports

When we turn the key in the ignition of a car, the first result is that a circuit opens from the battery to the starter motor. The battery then uses a mere 12 volts to push current to the starter motor, giving it enough "juice" to turn over.

As an economic metaphor, the battery is the source of the first exports. It is the stimulus for all subsequent activity. The money which flows into the local economy from those first exports is comparable to the current flowing from the 12-volt battery to the starter motor. It isn't much, but it makes all the difference, just as a small energy flow gives the starter motor the wherewithal to start the car.

The Alternator: Imports

Before looking more closely at what the starter motor does in economic terms, it's important to check out another part of this reciprocating system that also connects to the battery. This is the alternator. In a real engine, the alternator takes AC voltage from the electrical system, which is also reciprocating, and converts it to DC voltage. Once the engine is running, the alternator continues to provide current to the battery, replenishing its electrical energy.

As chapter 5 stated, no economy is self-sufficient. From the standpoint of the community's standard of living, the purpose of exports is to pay for the desired imports. Therefore, *if an economy stops importing, it loses the incentive to remain competitive with other economies.* This is why total self-sufficiency (autarky) is a policy for economic suicide.

In this sense, imports constitute the alternator, providing the motivation for the local economy to maintain exports by remaining competitive.

The Starter Motor: The Export Multiplier

Most people are familiar with the economic concept of the "multiplier effect." It's any given activity that generates positive side effects that become independent of that activity. The right combination of rabbits quickly illustrates the multiplier effect. So it is with economics, although less enjoyable for the participants.

Investment is the usual example of the multiplier effect. The economic development of Texas after the Civil War was largely the result of the railroads. Railroad construction created an enormous demand for lumber, for mule- and ox-teams, for grain to feed the animals and foodstuffs to feed the human work crews.

Railroads also made possible the shift in agriculture from subsistence farming to production for market. In Texas, unlike the rest of the South, cotton became "king" quite late, and only because of the railroads. The location of the rails also caused the creation of new cities.

The direct investment of millions of dollars in railroads caused tens of millions of dollars in other investments, and hundreds of millions of dollars in total economic activity.

This same effect exists in jobs. The oil industry, for example, created jobs in the industry itself, but many more jobs in peripheral industries that directly and indirectly serve the needs of oil-company employees: homebuilding, restaurants, movie theaters, schools, police and fire departments, retail outlets, insurance, and all the other services and products that people want. This too is well known. (Today, however, the oil-industry multiplier has become a divisor.)

But the "export multiplier," the term created by Jane Jacobs in *The Economy of Cities*, isn't as well known. It exists in the independent, local industries supplying inputs to exporting firms. The higher the ratio of independent local inputs to subsequent exports, the higher the export multiplier and therefore the more economic activity that results.

The export multiplier is the starter motor of economic development. Here is how it works.

In mass production industries, maximum specialization means maximum efficiency—and maximum profits. This specialization among employees is what the division of labor is all about.

Specialization provides maximum productivity, but also narrows the perspective. The function of the production people is routine. They may get a bonus for exceeding a production quota or for cutting costs, but they don't have an incentive to go out and find new customers or to come up with new uses for the firm's products. They certainly don't have any incentive to find ways to change a component. Everything is lock-step—nor should it be otherwise in a large vertically integrated firm in a well established industry.

However, a local entrepreneur, who can get a contract to supply inputs to an exporting firm that isn't part of a vertically integrated system, already has a production base to work with. If the local supplier's total sales are just a few million dollars a year, even a "mere" $100,000 in added sales is significant: The economies of scale will enable the entrepreneur to spread production costs over a wider production run, lowering unit costs. The profit margin on the extra $100,000 in sales will thus be higher than on previous sales of the same item.

Perhaps the exporting manufacturer wants a customized component. Then the entrepreneur must make an investment in new mental capital, and perhaps in new tangible assets, to provide the new component. To boost the return on that new investment, the entrepreneur will seek out more customers for that new component.

He or she will try to find new markets and new uses for the product, either as an input item or as a finished good in itself. And, if necessary, the entrepreneur will make further changes in the product in accordance with the specifications of other potential customers—as long as the net effect is to increase potential sales and profits. Any additional production will enable the manufacturer to ride the experience curve down to lower unit costs, while simultaneously building up mental capital.

This is not the sort of effort that one can expect from a branch plant that's part of a vertically integrated corporate network, but it's perfect for an entrepreneur. And the foregoing analysis would work just as well if the example involved a vendor of services rather than of tangible goods.

The result is that a local firm that starts by supplying inputs to another firm that's exporting can itself become an exporter eventually. If the original exporting firm is in a new industry, or is itself small enough so that it hasn't established vertical integration, then there are many opportunities for local firms to supply inputs and perhaps become exporters themselves someday.

The key factor here is that when many local firms can supply inputs, these firms have to compete with each other to provide quantitative and qualitative productivity improvements.

The development of the Houston economy is a good illustration. The city grew quite large, quite fast, during the post-1900 oil boom, in large part because the petroleum industry needed a lot of rigs, pipelines, tanks, and other inputs. The small oil firms couldn't provide these things for themselves, even if they had wanted to. The large oil firms could have, but fortunately for the future of Houston they decided to concentrate on what they did best, so they contracted with outside suppliers. But the technology and the manufactured equipment weren't imported. The Houston economy created and produced them. And Houston got the benefit—the chief one being that all of these firms, competing with each other, vastly improved their respective products.

Other cities around the world also were making oilfield equipment, but Houston's firms were able to provide a higher quality product or a lower price or better after-sales service or a combination of these, closer to the market. Houston's competitive edge resulted from mental capital and tacit knowledge. Its entrepreneurs destroyed their international rivals in the marketplace, and Houston became the drilling-technology capital of the world. That's the export multiplier at work.

Unfortunately, the rest of the story is that Houston then chose to rest on its laurels, and became "only" the drilling-technology capital of the world. In the same way Detroit—until recently—was "only" the auto-technology capital of the world. Who knows? The Japanese may yet do to Houston what they did to Detroit.

The Ignition Coil: The Import-Replacement Multiplier

This brings us to the ignition coil of an automobile engine. Like the starter motor, it also is "fed" by the current from the 12-volt battery. But the ignition coil is an amazing transformer that takes a small electrical input and turns it into nearly 10,000 volts of output. The electrical output from the ignition coil then flashes through the spark plugs and ignites the mixture of gasoline and air in the cylinders.

Most impressive is the fact that—in absolute terms, let alone relative terms—the ignition coil drains far less energy from the system than the starter motor does, even though the starter motor is in use for only a few seconds, whereas the ignition coil operates constantly once the engine starts.

Similarly, the export multiplier, akin to the starter motor, is much less energy efficient, and far less important, than the ignition coil. In this economic analogy, the ignition coil is what's called the "import-replacement multiplier," another concept and term from Jane Jacobs.

The import-replacement multiplier is no more familiar than the export multiplier. But if one pair of rabbits is the export multiplier, then the import-replacement multiplier is a Noah's Ark menagerie, happily procreating.

As the name implies, the import-replacement multiplier replaces imports with local production. The local economy thus creates new resources, new jobs, new cash flow, new profits, new tax revenues, and new wealth. This in turn pulls more people into active participation in the local economy. And this in turn creates even more demand for the peripheral activities mentioned in connection with the well-known investment multiplier. All of this, combined, further accelerates economic development. It's another virtuous circle, forming an upward spiral.

Just as the ignition coil takes a very small amount of electrical current and turns it into a very large electrical output, so the import-replacement multiplier can take a very small amount of economic input (the imports) and generate a huge amount of new local economic output by replacing the imports.

Import replacement is quite different from the familiar economic concept of import substitution. The distinction between the two is vital. Import substitution means the use of items that are already available, locally, as inferior surrogates for the desired imports. With import replacements, in contrast, there's a sincere lack of desire for the previous imports.

One example of import substitution occurred during the War of Northern Aggression. Texans made homespun clothes because the Yankee naval blockade shut off imports. This homespun was quite rough and not at all stylish, but it had to do. Likewise, most Texas cities today can't afford to import Dolly Parton or Placido Domingo more than once a year—if at all—and must make do with local talent.

The connotation of import substitution is one of reluctance. Import substitutes will not find an export market. Indeed, most people don't want them even in the local market. Import replacement, on the other hand, equals or surpasses the quality of the imports. Import replacements are not only welcome at home, they are sometimes welcomed elsewhere.

Most imports cannot be replaced. Usually, this is because the producers in another economy have too many advantages over the local economy. However, the real limiting factor on import replacement is the size of the local market for the imports in question. The potential for import replacement is determined by the economies of scale in the industry the imports come from.

If local demand for a given import is high enough, relative to the cost of production, then a local firm can begin making the item efficiently enough that it can compete effectively against the import—given the immediate advantage of lower transportation costs to reach the buyers.

Since Houston so often is used as the whipping boy for the sins of all Texas, this is a good place to give an example of how Houston did something right.

Contrary to propaganda that originates in certain other cities, Houston does have some "high technology" firms—Compaq, for one. However, when the first high-tech firms started in Houston, no continuing education was available locally for the electronics engineers who worked in them. These engineers either had to forego such training, or else had to take off from work and go out of town to get instruction on the latest technological developments in the industry.

Both alternatives served to impede the growth of Houston's high technology industry. With the latter alternative, Houston was, in effect, "importing" continuing education, because it was sending dollars out of the local economy to pay for education somewhere else.

One of the very last things that Dr. Norman Hackerman did before his retirement as president of Rice University was to start a program of continuing education there for electronics engineers. This killed two birds with one stone—or, should we say, put three eggs into a new nest?

First, Rice University replaced the former imports with local production of services. This kept funds in Houston that would otherwise have left.

Second, Rice University became an independent local supplier of inputs to the exports of Houston's high technology firms—in this case, indirect inputs of mental capital.

Third, Rice University might eventually bring in engineers from other economies, who heretofore had gone out of town for their continuing education just as Houston's engineers had done. Now, though, they'd be going to Houston instead of to their previous destinations. So Rice University would itself be "exporting" technical training, and the Houston economy would benefit from the inflow of funds.

However, this continuing education program at Rice University would not have been worth starting if the local market—previously served by imports—had not become large enough to justify the endeavor. Now that the program is successful, it provides what might be called an addition to the "intellectual infrastructure" of the Houston economy. It could have an incalculably stimulating effect on the further development of high-technology industries in Houston. Someday Dr. Hackerman's going-away present to his university may rank as one of the most significant acts of his entire career there.

Import replacement is so important, and apparently so little understood, that the next chapter is devoted entirely to it.

The Distributor: Financial Services
The 10,000 volts the ignition coil produces then go to the distributor. Comparing electrical current to cash flow: In a local economy the distributor is the financial system of banks, venture-capital firms, investment bankers, and other sources of money. The financial system distributes the seed capital, growth capital, and working capital to businesses, just as in a real engine the distributor channels current to the spark plugs.

Spark Plugs, Cylinders, Pistons ... and Value-Added
Business managers, especially entrepreneurs, are the spark plugs of the local economy. In an automobile, electricity flows through the spark plugs into the cylinders, where it ignites the mixture of fuel and air that has been compressed by the pistons. In this analogy, each cylinder represents a local firm, and the piston is the labor force. The explosion that takes place in the cylinder is the value-added.

The Crankshaft: The Economic Infrastructure
As mentioned, the starter motor takes current from the battery and converts this "juice" into mechanical energy to turn over the crankshaft. All of the pistons are connected to the crankshaft. If the starter motor is the export multiplier, the crankshaft is the economic infrastructure: the roads, rail lines, airports, office buildings, communications networks, and all other supporting systems and structures that make it possible for commerce to occur.

The starter motor is much less energy-efficient than the ignition coil. This is so in an economic engine, too, where the export multiplier is far less important than the import-replacement multiplier. It is much more difficult to set in motion any changes in the basic economic infrastructure than it is to create changes among the various firms.

In a real engine it is much harder to do the mechanical work of turning over a crankshaft than it is to transform 12 volts into nearly 10,000. So in the economic engine, it is much harder to build roads and new telephone networks than it is to start up a new firm or expand an old one.

Carburetor, Air Filter, Fuel Filter, and Radiator: The Rest of the Economic Engine
For those who want to see just how far this analogy can go in corresponding to reality ... the carburetor is the educational system. It combines the brains and character of the students with those of the teachers, along with the lessons of history and science. The air filter is the local government, especially the police force, keeping out the bad elements. The fuel filter is the state government, looking out for the interests of Texas. And the radiator is the national government, including the Federal Reserve System, supposedly keeping the economy from overheating.

Horsepower: Economic Abundance
We finally come to horsepower, which is what an engine is supposed to provide to those who want to go somewhere in life. Any given engine has only one battery, one starter motor, one ignition coil, one distributor, one crankshaft. But it can have any

number of cylinders, pistons, and spark plugs; the more the better, in terms of horsepower—and in terms of economic value-added.

A strong economy is a powerful engine. Economic development is the process of assembling a do-it-yourself engine and keeping it running well.

8 | Import Substitution vs. Import Replacement

Development is a do-it-yourself process; for any given economy, it is either do it yourself or don't develop.
—Jane Jacobs
Cities and the Wealth of Nations

It's a given that the world is interdependent. People talk of "economic globalization," including the growing role of America's international trade as a percentage of our gross national product and the need to promote more exports from the United States. Without doubt America—and Texas—needs to do something to boost exports (other than depreciating the exchange rate). But that is only the starting point, just as the export multiplier is only the starter motor of the economic engine, as we saw in the preceding chapter.

Trade occurs within any given economy, as well as between economies—be they local, regional, or national. And trade is not a "zero-sum game," where Peter gains what Paul loses, and vice versa—although it can be, depending on the terms of trade and the composition of the trade, as outlined in chapter 5.

Conventional wisdom regards all exports as good, and a trade surplus as very good. Yet the chapter on "Money vs. Wealth" showed that exports can actually be counterproductive, economically, and that a trade surplus in and of itself doesn't really mean much. The simplistic and emotional analysis of exports vs. imports tacitly assumes that all trade is a zero-sum game.

Protectionists who denounce imports point to the hardships caused by the demise of local firms. And, in the short run, those hardships are severe. In the long run, though, to stop importing would create far more hardships, because in a competitive world a high standard of living depends on free trade. Further, at least the hardships the protectionists complain about are localized. The hardships resulting from a noncompetitive economy based on import barriers would be far more widespread.

But even the free-trade people often miss the crucial point that the real purpose of exports is not that of promoting local economic growth via cash inflow. Such a doctrine is "neomercantilism" ("beggar thy neighbor"), just a mirror-reverse of protectionism. Exports may be the starting point for economic development, but they should not be the driving force once an economy has outgrown its infancy.

The real purpose of exports (which, by definition, have prevailed in the competition of the world's markets) is to provide the income to pay for imports—goods which other economies can produce more efficiently than the local economy. This in turn means that the people in the local economy don't have to pay as much for an item. If another economy can produce something more efficiently, then the local economy is maximizing its own efficiency by buying the import instead of producing the item locally. Because local people thus get more goods for their money, their standard of living is higher than it would be otherwise.

However, there are many situations where the local economy can itself produce an item that's being imported—and can do so with an efficiency that equals or surpasses that of an existing foreign producer, with no loss in quality. And, as the previous chapter indicated, it's this process of import replacement that is the vital factor in economic development.

Import substitution is a protectionist policy. It decreases an economy's efficiency. It's counterproductive. But import replacement serves to increase an economy's efficiency, because it means that an economy is investing in itself and expanding its internal trade in a cost/beneficial way.

A Word to the Wise
Skeptics may charge that import "substitution" vs. import "replacement" is merely a word game. However, import replacement actually serves to increase efficiency on a global scale.

It does this by providing genuine competition to the existing foreign suppliers. This in turn prods them to become more efficient. If they succeed, they maintain their current market share. In some cases, this might thwart the nascent competition from import replacement. And, if this happens, the new local producers fail.

With import substitution, the local producers will survive even if the foreigners become more efficient, because the local producers take advantage of a protected local market. But these local producers will never be able to reach out and challenge the foreign producers in other markets, because the locals won't be competitive.

With import replacement, based on free trade, even if the new local producers fail to survive, the overall local economy benefits. If the foreign producers do prevail over the new local competition, the local (importing) economy will find that the price of its imports has fallen, so both the importing economy and the exporting economy come out ahead—a "win/win" situation.

And, if the existing exporters cannot prevail over the local import replacements, then they at least will have been motivated to find ways to hang onto their market share in other markets, where they as yet have not been threatened with successful import replacement. The old exporters, of course, can anticipate that successful import replacements in one economy may eventually become successful exports to other economies—something that would never happen with mere import substitutes.

The fear of export competition from a former importer will thus cause a major exporter to find ways to give the remaining importers more for their money—while still making a good profit. Again, this is a win/win situation. It is what competition is all about, or should be.

Import substitution, on the other hand, is not competition. It's a "lose/lose" situation.

As long as free trade continues, attempts at import replacement will boost the productivity of all the participants. Import substitution, in contrast, will reduce the productivity of every participant. If existing exporters find an old market closed to them, they must spread their costs over reduced production runs. This increases unit costs, and reduces efficiency. It also, usually, results in a price increase.

Politically, import substitution is popular, because its positive impact on jobs, the trade balance, etc., is obvious. However, even though, in the short run, import substitution often seems beneficial to the protectionist economy, in the long run it diverts resources that could have been invested more productively in other industries.

Ironically, though, import substitution eventually reduces the protectionist economy's standard of living—or, at least, keeps it from improving as much as it would otherwise. This is because the hidden opportunity cost of protectionism vastly outweighs its benefits.

The biggest opportunity cost of protectionism is that it condemns an economy to perpetuating obsolete local industries. The industries themselves may not be obsolete, but if the local firms in those industries can't compete effectively in a free market, these firms are obsolete. Their resources, including what's left of their mental capital, are locked into substandard assets. They find themselves in an economic rut and will remain there, throwing good money after bad. It would be much better for them to accept their losses and free up resources for new endeavors that might enable them to more than make up the losses. Competition from the outside would force them to do this.

Import replacement, based on free trade, provides all the perceived benefits of import substitution but carries none of the hidden costs. And import replacement, being a free-market activity, does not give rise to the mutually parasitic relationships between special-interest groups, such as industries or labor unions, and the politicians who protect them.

Keep Your Eye on the Pie
Trade, in and of itself, is like that famous "economic pie" we all heard about in school. It keeps expanding so that everyone gets more pie than before, even if each person's share of the pie—in percentage terms—stays the same.

At the risk of sounding ridiculous, the relationship between external trade (both imports and exports) and internal trade is like that between the ice cream and the pastry in pie a la mode. Conventional wisdom focuses on the ice cream, but the really important thing is to keep your eye on the pie: the strictly local economy.

The pie keeps expanding as a result of import replacement and its multiplier effect. The process of import replacement generates enormous amounts of mental capital. And this mental capital in turn makes possible further development.

To change the metaphor, an economy becomes a breeder reactor, based on fusion, not fission.

With a high level of replacing imports, a local economy becomes vastly larger than the activity represented by its trade with other economies. The Japanese, for example, are fond of saying that they have to export in order to import, and they have to import in order to survive at all, since they have so few natural resources of their own.

However, because Japan clearly has the highest import-replacement multiplier in the world, Japan's internal economy is a much larger percentage of its gross national product than is the total economic activity represented by Japan's external trade. Granted, that's the pattern in most other countries, too. But the difference is that Japan's internal economy keeps growing largely by replacing imports.

This is the sign of a strong economy. The United States economy developed this way, too. But now the pattern here has reversed. The fact that the United States is becoming more active in world trade, as a *percentage* of our gross national product, is not a good sign at all, but a very bad one.

The effort to replace imports with genuinely competitive goods generates an enormous amount of mental capital. This mental capital leads to spin-offs, the creation of new goods that heretofore haven't existed in the world. These new products are then sold in the local market, and exported to other markets.

The money saved by replacing former imports and by selling new exports enables the local economy to buy still more imports and to eventually try to replace them, too. And so the process continues, an economic dynamo with increasing power. In absolute terms, trade grows. In relative terms, it diminishes, because the local economy grows even faster.

America isn't doing this anymore. Japan is. We are not renewing our mental capital through competitive advances. And so we're falling behind in creating new exports that would have favorable terms of trade and would thereby help us reverse the slow decline in our standard of living. The U.S.A. already is the world's largest debtor nation in terms of financial capital. Worse, we are gradually becoming a debtor nation in terms of mental capital. The more you use it, the more you have of it; and we aren't using it.

What's true for America in general is true for Texas in particular, but it's been true of Texas far longer than for the rest of America.

Exports are important because they pay for imports. So an economy must keep exporting competitive products. However, the most significant purpose of both exports and imports is that they provide an abundant supply of potential candidates for import replacement—which is to say, opportunities for a local economy to invest in itself.

This process doesn't reduce the local economy's imports. On the contrary, if exports expand, then imports should keep pace. It does change the composition of those imports, however. From the perspective of the statistician, the local economy is importing just as much as before, perhaps more. There's been no reduction in external trade.

What's happened is that some economies that had been exporting to this particular local economy suddenly find that they no longer have a market here for their products—not because of protectionism, but because the imports are no longer competitive. They lose, to be sure.

However, other economies have suddenly found an expanded market for their goods, because this local economy has shifted its imports, and is now buying from them. The money that's saved by not having to purchase former imports is then used to pay for these new and different imports. These new imports contribute to a rising standard of living for the people in the local economy. Far more important in the long run, they provide new candidates for import replacement. The Japanese understand this quite well.

An Import Replacement Scenario for Texas

A hypothetical scenario illustrates this process with respect to

Texas:

Texas imports silks from China. But then Dow Chemical's researchers in Texas develop a petrochemical-based fiber that looks and feels just like Chinese Shantung silk. Only an expert can tell the difference. Dow then produces this material in Lake Jackson, Texas. Soon Dallas apparel companies are turning out garments that look and feel like silk, but cost much less. The Chinese no longer have a good market in Texas.

The Texas economy has conserved its money, no longer sending it to the Chinese economy. The Texas economy also has created new wealth, in the form of the production facilities and people at work in Lake Jackson and Dallas. And, since the new "silk" garments are competitive, the Texas economy starts exporting them to other economies, thereby generating even more revenues, more local jobs, and all the other benefits of economic development.

But it doesn't stop there. Texas has more money to spend than before: the money saved, the new wealth created internally, and the revenues from new exports. So Texans start importing more luxuries, such as wines from France, Germany, California, and New York.

Yet Texas vintners are at work, producing Texas wines that are better than all but the very best of the imports. Soon the French, Germans, Californians, and New Yorkers find that their sales in Texas have fallen off. And the Texas wines are so good they begin to be exported. This means that these other vintners find that their sales are falling off in markets other than Texas, due to competition from former customers in Texas.

Once again, Texas harvests a double benefit: It keeps funds in the local economy, and brings in more funds from other economies via exports.

Another, final, round illustrates the process further. Texans then use some of this new-found money supply to start importing video games from Japan as gifts for their children. Pretty soon Texas parents realize that these games are more than just a fad: The games are addictive, expensive (with an endless supply of "new, improved" versions), and idiotic.

But at last a couple of software "whiz kids" get together in San Antonio and create a new video game. This new game is not idiotic, it's educational. Although it too is addictive, its effect is to addict children to learning things of value. Of course, the two software creators are not fools; they also produce a series of "new, improved" versions, in different subjects. The new games are manufactured in Austin and become popular not only in Texas but all around the world, as the Texas company even starts creating versions in foreign languages.

The point to keep in mind is that, in each case, the level of external economic activity has remained in balance. There is no trade deficit or surplus. What comes in from selling more exports is used to buy more imports. It's quite likely that the level of external economic activity has grown, in absolute terms. However, the internal economic activity has grown enormously, both in absolute terms and as a percentage of total economic activity. That's import replacement at work. And because of the import-replacement multiplier, the replacement of former imports with local production has generated the huge increase in peripheral activities that all local economies require.

There is yet another benefit of great importance that accrues from replacing imports: If it should happen that significant export markets—or prices—for Texas products should suddenly collapse, then prior rounds of import replacement would make Texas less dependent on the need to generate new exports immediately. At such a time, most imports would be luxury goods, more or less. Even with the collapse of exports, there would still be enough goods going out to pay for those imports which are absolute necessities. And the mental capital built up from prior import replacement would give Texas a much better chance of generating the new exports to exchange for the desired luxury imports.

In chapter 6, mental capital was compared, in passing, to an economic insurance policy against disaster. It's import replacement that enables an economy to pay the premiums on that policy.

The key to a sound economic policy, and to a long-run increase in our standard of living, is the import-replacement multiplier. Although the examples given relate mostly to foreign products, the same process is vital to trade within Texas, because each local economy essentially is on its own, regardless of the political entity of which it officially is a part.

Branch Plants: Short End of the Stick

There are various ways to replace imports. Unfortunately, the easiest is also the worst: the branch plant. There are several reasons why this is so.

First, because a branch plant is built to fulfill a supply role within a worldwide system, corporate headquarters has already decided how large an area, how big a market, the plant will serve.

No entrepreneur, just starting up, would ever accept being told that he or she will not be allowed to exceed X dollars in sales per year. Yet this is what happens when a branch factory is built. While the new economic activity from a branch plant may be better than no new economic activity at all, it still provides the lowest potential for future expansion of the local economy. What seems so productive actually is sterile.

Granted, other plants might be closed down elsewhere, or the new plant in Texas could later be enlarged to supply increased market demand. But even so, there is an inevitable constraint—which has been predetermined. The factory may suddenly thrust upward from the local economic landscape, but it will always be a mesa, never a mountain.

Second, a branch plant is part of a highly coordinated, but highly fragmented, operation. A branch plant is a production facility and nothing more. Division of labor exists not only on the shop floor, but throughout a corporation that has a network of branch plants. Research facilities are in one location, financial activities in another, and so on.

The person in charge of local production is an important official in the company and very capable, but he or she is not a well-rounded executive. The people under the production manager are also specialized, with few if any opportunities to interface with people in other roles. The effect of all this is to minimize the potential for entrepreneurial spin-offs from the factory.

In the discussion of the export multiplier, the main point was that local independent suppliers of inputs could eventually become exporters themselves. They have every incentive to do so. This is largely because the entrepreneurs who are independent suppliers are able to look at "the big picture" of the entire market and their firms.

With a branch-factory operation, even if some determined

individual has somehow managed to see the big picture, he or she is still all alone. This in itself makes seed capital more difficult to come by. But even if it's available, the entrepreneur must still round up a "team" of strangers.

Most spin-offs involve teamwork. Men and women with different specialties have worked together and developed respect for and trust in one another. They are confident that they can work well together, which gives their new company an added chance for success.

It's often said that pioneers end up full of arrows. In large part, this is because a pioneer is out there on his or her own, and has to try to cover everything at once until he or she gets enough money together to hire good teammates. But in a new company even a team takes a while to develop working relationships, whether or not they've worked together before, because now they're out in the economic wilderness—and under attack from corporate Comanches.

This is just a metaphor, but those who've had real combat experience know that very often the difference between being "V.F.W." (a member of the Veterans of Foreign Wars) and "K.I.A." (killed in action) depends on the presence of buddies you know you can trust with your very life. It isn't so different in business, although "R.I.P." (rest in peace) usually is inscribed only on a corporate tombstone, rather than a personal one, in the case of failure.

Texas Instruments has probably been the prime source in our state for entrepreneurial spin-offs. This isn't due solely to TI's informal atmosphere for management personnel. More important is that TI's organization provides a rich mix of specialists in most locations who have a chance to see the big picture, compare notes, and build up their own informal networks before spinning off.

The bigger TI becomes, and the more fragmented its parts, the less this can happen. This reduces the likelihood of entrepreneurial spin-offs and increases the odds against those who do leave. It also limits the potential of those who would never leave anyway. Still, the Texas economy can best protect its future by encouraging home-grown import replacements rather than by "importing" a branch plant of a firm that had previously been "exporting" to Texas.

The third reason why a branch factory is the least desirable means of replacing imports is that a branch factory is exclusively a production facility. The mental capital of the firm usually remains at headquarters. The capital equipment is brought in as part of an industrial engineering plan that's already been worked out in as much detail as the corporate marketing and logistics plans for the factory's output.

"Quality Control circles" and the development of "tacit knowledge" can always find some way to improve things even more, of course. But what then happens is that this new mental capital (and it most definitely is that) quickly gets sent to the home office for sharing with all the other branch plants.

So branch operations offer no competitive advantage for the Texas economy. If the branch plant were, instead, the factory of an independent local firm, each improvement would immediately give the Texas company an edge over its competition in other cities, states, and countries.

If the major Texas producers of oilfield technology had just been branch plants of some nationwide or multinational operation, then it's almost certain that Pittsburgh or Cleveland would still be the center of such technology today.

We've all heard the saying, "If you give a man a fish, you feed him for a day; if you teach him how to fish, he can feed himself for a lifetime." For a small town, a branch factory, or even the presence of several branch factories, is fishy.

What counts is the ratio of the branch plant's activity to the total activity of the economy; the impact of the investment and jobs multiplier needs to be included. An economy that is dependent on a branch plant is like the man who's been given the fish, but who continues to get a fish day after day. If the corporate headquarters later decides to take the fish away, the town is in serious trouble—as Carrollton, Texas, discovered when both Apple Computer and Mostek suspended their operations there, without warning.

For a large economy, however, a branch plant, on balance, can be a good thing. This is especially true if the local economy has a high level of mental capital and a high import-replacement multiplier. Such an economy already has real wealth; it is already independent. To use the buzzwords of financial analysis, the upside (potential gain) is nice, while the downside (the risk of losing its contribution to the economy) doesn't jeopardize the entire stability of the local economy. In terms of the fishing analogy, a large, healthy economy already knows how to fish. It even has its own poles. The branch plant provides new bait with which to catch more dollars.

Further, even though a branch factory discourages spin-offs and entrepreneurship, in a large economy there are a whole lot of people who would never want to become entrepreneurs. A branch plant is a good place for them to work. In a small economy, though, the branch plant can easily soak up all the ambitious and talented people around: people who would otherwise start their own truly independent businesses in the local economy, or else would leave for the big city where they could make a greater contribution and obtain greater rewards.

This question of scale, of the ratio between dependent and independent activity, is no different when considering branch plants than it was when considering exports. The more an economy is dependent on the outside world, the weaker it is.

Even though a branch factory is part of the local economy, that local economy is still dependent on decisions made by the outside world of corporate headquarters concerning the future of that plant. Those outsider executives can never know the local situation, and its future potential, as well as the local people do. Distant financial analysts will make a cold-blooded assessment that can literally mean life or death for some people.

But all the outsiders have to go on are pages of computer print-outs filled with numbers, and perhaps a quick visit to the branch factory. They're not even aware of the intangible factors that can make such a difference in the future. And they couldn't begin to accurately weigh those factors even if they were aware of them. The local economy is at their mercy.

The less pivotal any given business or industry is to a local economy, the better off that economy is. This is especially true with branch plants. So, while this may sound like "sour grapes," it's probably a blessing in disguise that small Texas cities lost out in the competition a few years ago to become the site of the General Motors Saturn Corporation facilities.

As with protectionism, a branch plant provides obvious short-term benefits. However, also as with protectionism, it has hidden long-term costs: the preordained production constraint, the discouragement of entrepreneurial spin-offs, the loss of a competitive advantage from the creation of new mental capital. All of these are opportunity costs. These harmful consequences eventually subvert and destroy the short-term gains the branch plant offers to smaller communities.

Imitation as Self-Obliteration

There's another relatively unsatisfactory way to create import replacements. This involves a full-scale imitation of the way things already are being done elsewhere. For example, a group of Texas financiers could decide that the Lone Star State should be producing its own farm implements instead of importing them from, say, Chicago, Illinois, or Racine, Wisconsin. These financiers could form a corporation, fund it with millions of dollars, hire industrial engineers to design a plant that uses the latest technology, retain experienced executives from farm-implement manufacturers, recruit a local labor force, and set them all to work.

Good luck. In theory, a new factory, using the latest production technology, can achieve some cost advantage over its competitors. But any new company that jumps into an industry with a full-blown enterprise built from scratch is asking for trouble.

Other firms that have been in the business for a long time have certain advantages in the marketplace to offset at least some of the price disadvantage. A new firm that tries to challenge them head-on will be short on those advantages, and especially short on mental capital. It can hire some of the top people in the industry, but it still must recruit a labor force, however small, that is completely inexperienced. This approach is an invitation to financial disaster.

The people of Fort Worth tried this with meatpacking in 1885. The city gave $75,000 to a company to help defray the cost of buying land and building a plant. The firm obtained a contract to supply a large quantity of dressed beef to the English market. On the strength of that contract, Fort Worth put up another

$40,000 to bring the plant into production. But the local managers and labor force just couldn't work the "bugs" out of the system. The factory was idled.

A few years later Fort Worth tried again, this time with half a million dollars. The factory came on stream, but it was never able to hold its costs down enough to compete in markets beyond the immediate area. It kept losing money, and by the turn of the century it had shut down permanently. Eventually, the Chicago firm of Swift & Company built a branch plant in Fort Worth and established it as a meatpacking center.

Imitation may be the sincerest form of flattery, but it can also be the worst form of self-inflicted battery.

In Search of the Competitive Edge

What's missing in these examples is the competitive edge. That edge usually is developed by taking on just one small part of a large market or a large industry, and then moving forward one step at a time from there.

Titan Aerospace is an excellent example of how to do it right. Brian Byers used to be an airplane broker, serving the south and central African market. Kenneth Vornsand ran a construction business in Houston. They knew each other. They also knew that Cessna Aircraft, of Wichita, Kansas, had discontinued production of the Cessna 404.

This plane has enough room to carry fourteen passengers or a lot of cargo. However, it's powered by piston engines, so a fully loaded Cessna 404 can't get off the ground. A most interesting oversight—which the two men noted. They regarded the 404 as a Cadillac with a Volkswagen engine, and decided to do something about it.

Byers and Vornsand readily acknowledged their lack of capital, both financial and mental. So they certainly couldn't challenge Cessna directly. Instead, they found a market niche in corporate aircraft, using the Cessna 404 itself. Byers and Vornsand knew that there were roughly 400 of the planes in corporate hands. Their market consisted of the Cessna 404 owners who wanted to upgrade the aircraft's capabilities.

The two men formed Titan Aviation (now Titan Aerospace), a Houston-based service business. They take the Cessna 404s, and yank the piston engines out. Then they replace them with Pratt & Whitney propjet engines, made in Canada, which cost $400,000. (Titan doesn't buy these engines without a firm order in hand!)

The labor is performed at established aviation mechanical-service centers. Titan doesn't own these centers, nor does it want to. This way it doesn't have to foot the bill for the overhead and labor force. Labor cost to customers for the conversion is $225,000. If the customer doesn't already own a Cessna 404, Titan can supply one, conversion included, for $850,000.

Again acknowledging their lack of sufficient resources, the founders of Titan contracted with an airplane broker in Washington, D.C., to market the plane outside the U.S.A. They've renamed the (converted) Cessna 404, calling it the Omni Turbo Titan, partly in recognition of the brokering firm, Omni International. However, 85 percent of the world market for corporate aircraft is within the U.S.A., and Titan can handle this market.

In short, Titan Aerospace caught Cessna napping, and took advantage of it in a small way. It wasn't exactly David challenging Goliath, because Titan wasn't trying to shoot Cessna down. However, what made the minor injury a major insult to Cessna was that David was using Goliath's own sling, Cessna's old planes, to take business away from Cessna's sale of new planes.

Cessna soon woke up and decided to produce its own propjet aircraft. This is called the Cessna 406. However, the Wichita, Kansas, folks couldn't come up with enough mental capital of their own to meet their new competition: The 406 will carry only nine passengers instead of the Omni Turbo Titan's 14. It uses Polish engines instead of Pratt & Whitney's, which could mean limited service locations. It's been certified only in France.

Worst of all, the Cessna 406 costs $1.3 million, nearly half a million more than the Texans charge for an Omni Turbo Titan. Even though Cessna was subsequently acquired by General Dynamics, that Goliath's muscle was not enough to crush the nimble upstart.

Titan Aerospace doesn't make aircraft or engines. It's a service business. But if Cessna doesn't regain its competitiveness, the Omni Turbo Titan may yet provide the cornerstone for a civilian-aircraft manufacturing facility on a large scale in Texas. Only time will tell. (And note the Texas bravado: "Titan," "Aerospace," indeed!)

Skeptics will comment that, despite the name, Titan Aerospace is unlikely to ever become an important part of the Texas economy. True. It's also true that the oil bust has hurt Titan's sales more than the response from Cessna ever could have.

However, Titan, along with tens of thousands of other small firms, collectively can make an enormous impact on the Texas economy. More important to the future of this state, such firms are "home grown" and not dependent on the perceptions and decisions of executives whose offices are thousands of miles from the Lone Star State.

Texas boosters grouse that New York State spends $60 million a year to promote itself—and the State of Illinois allegedly spends $200 million. But the Texas expression, "It ain't braggin' if you do it," seems appropriate here. If we're going to brag about how wonderful Texas is for business, shouldn't we prove it here first? Why can't we just do it, and let the facts speak for themselves? If Texas is so good for business, we shouldn't have to beg corporations to relocate their headquarters here or to build branch plants here.

The best advertising is word-of-mouth. Business executives accord much more credibility to a few off-the-cuff remarks by a fellow executive than they do to all the slick brochures, videos, and "dog and pony" shows that government and chamber of commerce officials present. On a cost/benefit basis, the power of example is much more effective than even the best propaganda.

Anyone who's ever negotiated knows that the person who can sincerely say (or at least successfully bluff), "I don't need you as much as you need me," has the upper hand. But we Texans seem to feel that we just can't make it on our own. So when our leaders negotiate with outside firms, they often end up giving away all sorts of goodies that provide these outsiders with a competitive advantage over the local firms that have been here all along, through thick and thin. What sense does such a giveaway program make, in the long run?

There may be more glamour and more self-satisfaction in seeing a huge branch plant where there had been nothing before.

But an economy's continuing health depends on the relatively small, completely local, businesses. These are the businesses that have the most to gain from replacing imports.

As the saying goes, "If wishes were horses, beggars would ride." Empty public relations campaigns prove only that if hype were reality, all the hot air involved in these efforts would give us a new source of natural gas for the Texas energy industry.

9 | Certainty vs. Risk

> *The principle of bottom-up marketing is simple: you work from the specific to the general, from the short term to the long term . . . The fatal flaw in many marketing plans is a strategy based on "predicting the future." . . . The most common flaw is extrapolating a trend.*
>
> —Al Ries and Jack Trout
> *Bottom-Up Marketing*

American corporations have been justly accused of not taking a long-term approach. Instead, they focus on sales and earnings on a quarter-by-quarter basis. Critics have noted that the Japanese take a long-term approach, building market share and a reputation for product quality. The Japanese know that taking marginal profits or even losses in the short run will enable them to create a "cash cow" in the long run, if they succeed in capturing a large market share based on a reputation for high quality and a good price.

To some extent, the difference in approach is based on fundamental differences between the way Japanese and American corporations are financed, and on the way in which Japanese and American managers gain promotions. This is not the place to go into a detailed discussion of those differences. Unfortunately, Japanese corporations have some inherent advantages in these matters that American corporations simply cannot overcome, given our present system. Yet it is possible for American firms to do more by way of long-term thinking, and some American managers have begun to do just that. As often happens, though, a good idea becomes distorted in its application and counterproductive in its results.

We Americans pride ourselves on our pragmatism. If something isn't working out, we're often quick to discard it and try something else.

This is most obvious in politics. If things aren't going well for us when one party is in office, we blame the malaise on that party's principles and vote that party's officeholders out. We seem to believe that the incumbents' principles have been proven wrong somehow, and by implication the challengers' principles might be right—or at least worth a chance.

In economics, as in politics, we have little patience for examining fundamental principles. Even less do we consider the possibility that failure has resulted from the policies chosen to implement principles, rather than from the principles themselves. And so, too often, we throw the baby out with the bathwater.

Now that we've begun to recognize the need for a long-term approach, "grand strategy" has become the rage. Strategic thinking is a valuable activity. But what's happening in practice is that our strategic thinking involves a retreat to the ivory tower.

The real key to Japan's success is that the Japanese have concentrated on creating wealth instead of just making money. American managers and financiers, on the other hand, concentrate on mere paper profits. Somewhere out there in the real world there are real assets. But these real assets, and their potential to create real wealth, are rapidly dwindling as our business "hot shots" shove pieces of paper around and pile up huge "financial gains."

This is where labels such as "short term" vs. "long term" become a disservice. The main flaw in America's short-term focus is that it is strictly financial. It does not deal with the real world in terms of wealth, but only in terms of money. The "grand strategy" approach correctly shifts the emphasis to the long term, but then proves counterproductive by virtually ignoring the real world of the here and now in favor of what may well prove to be only blue sky.

Another part of the American problem is our emphasis on macroeconomics. "Big picture" thinking naturally follows from this. There's nothing wrong with trying to see the big picture. But, as noted in chapter 4, too often this approach misses the trees and sees only the forest. Granted, the present alternative—microeconomics—looks only at the trees, and only at one at a time.

That won't do either, obviously.

We need to create a third alternative: mesoeconomics. We need to ask, "Where does the forest come from?" "Where do the seedlings come from?" We also must ask how a given collection of seedlings can grow and attain the "critical mass" necessary to become a vibrant forest.

The main problem with the "grand strategy" approach, as practiced, is that it's a "top-down" approach. Also, as practiced, it's a luxury available only to those managers whose firms are large enough to be able to spare funds for personnel and person-hours for "strategic thinking" as an act in itself, isolated from the give and take of daily demands on the shop floor and in the marketplace. As such, it's clearly an activity for big business, big government, and big academia.

Yet these are the very people who are most out of touch with what's happening in the real world. These are also the very people whose perceptions of the future are shaped mostly by what they read in the press or see on television, rather than by their own experiences on the firing line.

People in big business, especially, tend to be hostile toward the media. They rightly note that most reporters don't seem to understand business, have little or no worthwhile business experience, and in general seem to have a prejudice against capitalism. But these very same big-businesspeople then turn around and base most of their own long-term thinking on what the media say the future will be like.

This is the "megatrends" approach, which has become quite a fad among people in big business, government, and academie. The irony is wonderful, but its consequences could prove disastrous.

Alvin Toffler and John Naisbitt are the most celebrated gurus among "futurists." Both have provided much food for thought. Yet both claimed certainty for their predictions, and far too many "opinion leaders" took those claims at face value.

Business writers, including the author of this book, are selling ideas. The potential customers for those ideas usually are businesspeople. When a salesperson calls on a potential customer to tout a new product or service, the wise businessperson takes the claims with a grain of salt. Even if the customer buys, the first order is usually small and the goods or services are thoroughly tested before the customer follows through with a large order. But when someone selling ideas comes along, businesspeople prove all too gullible, all too often.

Alvin Toffler's reputation is based on his discussion of what he called the "future shock" syndrome. Later, he turned the negative of future shock into the positive of "the third wave."

In between the two books with those respective titles, he did a slim volume called *Ecospasm*. This book quickly disappeared and is not remembered today. Toffler, for one, would prefer that it remain forgotten, and for good reason: It quickly became obvious that he was completely wrong in his analysis and predictions. Granted, *Future Shock* and *The Third Wave*, in contrast, had a lot of valuable material in them. But that hardly justifies taking everything in them as gospel.

The case of John Naisbitt is even more extraordinary. At least Toffler had a track record as an editor at *Fortune*, the prestigious business magazine. Naisbitt, on the other hand, has been exposed for falsifying virtually his entire background. Yet his reputation has continued to increase, at least among those businesspeople who like to be trendy.

Worse, all of Naisbitt's "megatrends" were based on mere extrapolations of patterns he claimed to discern from reading newspapers. But anyone who's ever been a reporter knows that there is a "group think" mentality at work in the press. The "news" is what news reporters and editors say it is. If something doesn't get publicity, then by definition it isn't news.

Furthermore, the "news" is a business. Because the news media allegedly describe reality, we forget that the publication we're reading, or the program we're watching or listening to, has to deliver an audience in order to stay in business. The news media sell news in the same way that businesspeople sell products or services. Even non-profit news operations, which rely on contributions or tax dollars, still must gain a respectable audience share to prove they're worthy of further financial support.

Most potential customers of products and services have a pretty good idea of whether or not they need a given product or service. With the news, it's different. If all the news media are reporting something as being supposedly important for their readers, listeners, or viewers, then the customer would have to respond with a block of salt to question that judgement.

But while the news business is a service, particular news items are products. And if a given news item proves a good sell for one news organization, similar items will prove a good sell for other news organizations.

This explains a lot of the public hysteria regarding AIDS. Before AIDS, it was the herpes scare. What ever happened to herpes? It's still out there, and still an epidemic. But the media found something that would sell even better in this "product category," and dropped herpes in favor of AIDS.

The media cycle news in much the same way as the music industry cycles "Top 40" records. If something starts moving, everyone wants to get in on the action.

As Al Ries and Jack Trout said in their book, *Bottom-Up Marketing* (1989):

> What do you think editors and reporters read? That's right, the output of other editors and reporters. It's a great deal easier than generating original material... The reality never seems to catch up with the hype. The future always seems to be just over the next hill.

It's also a lot easier for businesspeople to read the output of editors and reporters than it is to generate original material. What results is a bandwagon effect, a so-called "self-fulfilling prophecy."

Businesspeople often distrust the media with regard to political news, and with regard to news that directly concerns their own immediate industry. However, they lend amazing credence to news reports of matters that they don't have the time to check out for themselves but which seem important.

These matters, these "megatrends," seem important because the media say they're important. But all too often the media simply don't understand what they're talking about—and don't really care. After all, they're in business to make money too, and if a given line of news "works" in generating revenues, then why fix it?

But the credibility of the news media has a more sinister effect. Large businesses, for example, have the resources to commission their own studies of what appear to be trends in the making. But if the media have already declared the truth of a trend, it would take a courageous researcher to buck that alleged trend. What usually happens, instead, is that the resulting research report hedges the bet. This is the well-known practice of "C.M.A." (cover my anatomy).

Two quick examples will suffice. Both concern Japan. First, it's said that the Japanese have a much higher savings rate than we do. Second, it's said that the Japanese never take days off from work, not even vacations to which they're entitled.

The first statement is true. But no one ever bothers to explain, or to look into, the reason. Part of it is that there is virtually no consumer installment credit in Japan, not even mortgages. If a Japanese wants to buy a new refrigerator, a new car, or a new house, the only way to do it is to save until he or she has the purchase price.

Also, there are no corporate pensions in Japan, and no social security system. If a Japanese wants to provide for his or her old age, such provision must come out of personal savings.

This changes the picture, doesn't it?

The second statement, about the Japanese as "workaholics," is false. True, the Japanese don't take the personal vacations to which they're entitled. But the reason is that Japan has more mandatory national holidays than any other advanced industrial nation, including two consecutive weeks at New Year's.

Further, each Japanese is expected to take days off to participate in the reunion at his or her ancestral village every year. The villages schedule these reunions at different times.

Each employer knows that when a given employee's village holds its reunion, that employee has to be there—even if the village is on the other side of Japan. This is a very important custom, and everyone honors it.

So much for Japan's workforce as drone bees who labor without rest.

The problem of our gullibility isn't the media. The problem is with those who ought to know better, or who ought at least to suspect they aren't getting the truth, the whole truth, and nothing but the truth from the media.

Individual news items, or the existence of an apparent pattern of unfolding events, might well be worth further investigation. But to claim a "megatrend" or a "third wave" exists, simply because of a collection of news items, is folly.

Just because the media say something is so doesn't mean that it is so—although it might be. The farther news reports get away from specific events, the more likely it is that their analyses will be inaccurate.

The main item on the futurist agenda is high technology. "High tech" is vital to our future, to be sure. However, while it is necessary, it is not sufficient. And it definitely is not the solution to our economic problems here in Texas. Helpful, yes, but hardly the cure-all it's claimed to be.

The high-technology segment of the national economy and of the Texas economy is quite small. And it's going to stay small. The Bureau of Labor Statistics, for example, says that high-tech represents less than 3 percent of all employment. Peter Drucker, in his book *Innovation and Entrepreneurship*, estimates that, in the past twenty years, only one job out of every eight new jobs was in the high-tech sector. He went on to say that only one-fourth of the fastest-growing companies in America are in high technology.

It's wonderful that Texas is the site of the Microelectronics and Computer Technology Corporation, of Sematech, and of the future "supercollider." We also need to do more to turn at least some of our universities into first-rate centers of high-tech research and development. (The University of Houston is off to a good start with Dr. Paul Chu's work on superconductivity.)

However, Texas already has a lot of competition in high technology. Many of our competitors are far ahead of us in converting academic research and development into marketable products and successful firms. We need to stay in this race and improve our performance. However, even if we win it, the Texas economy will not be transformed.

A military analogy might be helpful here. In some circumstances, a given weapon might be absolutely essential, perhaps even literally a matter of life and death. If you have it, you live because you can deal with the threat. If you don't, you succumb. But no military force uses only one weapon, or bases its entire strategy and all of its tactics on the possession of any one weapon or weapons system.

What counts is flexibility, and that means a wide array of weapons—and skills. The more exotic weapons and the more glamorous skills are those used least often in a full-scale war. Most of the fighting is done by the lowly infantry, using standard-issue firearms.

Al Ries and Jack Trout, in their books on marketing, are quite fond of military analogies. In the following passages from *Bottom Up Marketing*, they're speaking of business executives, but their words also apply to current Texas efforts at economic recovery:

> Their strategy often consists of trying to do the same as the leader in the category but only a little bit better. It's like a general saying that all we have to do is fight a little harder wherever we choose to fight and everything will work out.
>
> On business battlefields, head honchos would rather hang in there and slug it out. They believe in an "all we need is a better effort" strategy ... A "can do" attitude gets high marks in the corporation, while "defeatists" are tagged as poor team players and given low marks.

No doubt *Rx for Texas* will be condemned by many for allegedly having a "defeatist" attitude. However, it would be more accurate to call it a "practical" attitude. Fighting hard, like working hard, is a good thing. But it's much better to fight, and to work, smart. And one of the best ways to fight and work smart is to start by questioning the conventional wisdom, the "group think" mentality.

There are 15,000 local, state, and regional economic-development agencies in America, all trying to do exactly the same thing as many Texans are. Instead of going with the herd and merely trying to do a better job of "me, too!," we might consider trying some rugged individualism instead.

Investigating the Mysteries

Burton H. Klein is an economist who recently retired from the California Institute of Technology. (He is not to be confused with Laurence S. Klein, the econometrician at the University of Penn-

94 • RX FOR TEXAS

sylvania who created the "Wharton Model" of the U.S. economy.) In 1977, Burton Klein's book, *Dynamic Economics*, was published. In it, he grappled with three "mysteries" of economic history, as he called them.

The first was the "growth paradox." The conventional wisdom of economic theory had said that a nation's initial economic progress depends on thrift and capital accumulation. But in 1956 it was discovered that this had not been the case for America's development. Although the economists accepted this revelation as valid, they could not explain it. Hence, the name "growth paradox."

So, to this day, professors teach the conventional wisdom in colleges and in economics graduate programs. Professional economists give advice to the government based on a theory that long ago lost its claim to explain reality.

But that doesn't stop officials from complaining that our economic problems are largely caused by American consumers and their credit-card indebtedness. People at the highest levels of government and the economics profession solemnly allude to the fable of "The Grasshopper and the Ant," in which the grasshopper lived for today and the ant saved for tomorrow, with a predictable moralistic outcome. Such thinking enabled the banking industry to demand—and get—subsidies such as the legislation for Individual Retirement Accounts. But savings do not necessarily become worthwhile investments, as the subsequent use of funds by the banking industry has clearly demonstrated.

The second mystery Klein studied was the "trade paradox," also disclosed in 1956. Conventional wisdom had long held that, as America developed, we shifted our trade patterns. Originally, it was said, we'd imported capital-intensive products and exported labor-intensive products. Then, as the Industrial Revolution spread through the United States, the pattern reversed, staying that way ever since (at least, until 1956).

But the new research indicated the existence of a "trade cycle." The exports from the United States throughout our history were usually products based on new technologies. As these technologies matured, other countries began to produce the goods in question more cheaply than we could. Then Americans began to import these items, instead of exporting them. In the meantime, we had shifted our exports to goods based on still-newer technologies.

Again, the economists accepted the validity of the report. Again, the economists could not explain the situation. And so, again, they continued—and still continue—to teach the obsolete theory of trade to future economists, businesspeople, and government leaders. It is called the "theory of comparative advantage," based on "relative factor endowments," more formally known as the Hoeksher-Olim Theorem.

Granted, economists have laid on a veneer of updated "factors" such as what in this book is called "mental capital," including organizational skills. But these additions can explain what happened only after the fact, and thus are useless in analyzing the potential of an economy that seemingly lacks these new factors. The revised theory still cannot explain economic development in Japan.

Today our vested interests decry the "exploitation of cheap labor" by foreign manufacturers. They claim that for America to import what it previously exported is a bizarre distortion of the norm. This is simply not so. What is a bizarre distortion, though, is America's failure to maintain its leadership in creating and exporting goods based on new technologies.

In fact, Klein's third "mystery" is America's loss of technological leadership. His book was an effort to explain the mysteries. He concluded that, for the United States:

> "... the United States did not become a technological leader in order to enjoy an export surplus. Technological leadership occurred as a *by-product* of its efforts to improve *productivity*."

Europe, in contrast, valued technological innovation for its own sake, as though research and development were an artistic endeavor. European firms would make wonderful discoveries, but then fail to follow through in a practical way. State-of-the-art products developed there simply cost too much relative to the benefits they imparted. Americans did not make this mistake.

This brings us back to mental capital. New invention by itself is not enough. New invention must withstand the test of the marketplace. New technology must not only do the job it's designed to do, it must do it more cheaply than the existing technology. In short, capitalism and competition are inseparable from mental capital.

Klein also commented:

> To explain what makes countries either good generators or good borrowers of technological ideas is a question that must be answered at the level of the firm.

The firm that provides an innovation that improves its productivity can ride the experience curve downward at a faster rate than its competition. It might even open up a new market, giving it a further competitive edge.

In explaining the mysteries that other economists still choose to sweep under the carpet, Klein—not surprisingly—had to challenge the conventional wisdom of economics.

The theories of John Maynard Keynes have dominated economics for more than fifty years now. Liberal economists such as John K. Galbraith and conservative economists such as Milton Friedman all base their own work, and their own recommendations, on Keynes.

In his most important book, *The General Theory*, Keynes stated the intellectual assumptions that were his starting point:

> We take as givens the existing skill and quantity of labor available, the existing quantity and quality of equipment, the degree of competition, and the habits of the consumer.

In short, Keynes chose to ignore the most important aspect of capitalism: change. Burton Klein, in contrast, soon realized that the process of capitalism as a means of economic transformation was far more important than the strictly monetary and budgetary statistics that Keynes discussed. As Klein noted:

> The classical theory of competition cannot explain how progress comes about, because it is premised on the assumption of a completely static world in which firms act on the basis of perfect knowledge. Indeed, if firms acted as if their knowledge were complete, no progress could ever occur!

Klein discerned that the key factor in competition is that firms try to improve productivity as a way of boosting their profit margins or market shares. But firms have many options as to how to boost their productivity. And therein lies the problem. Klein says:

> If a firm should decide to bring about minor advances when its competition is engaged in bringing about major advances it would risk going out of business. However, it would also risk going out of business if it failed to recognize that its ability to cope with uncertainty is limited.

The level of uncertainty is the controlling factor. A firm or an entire economy can go "all out" in one direction, and even be fairly confident that the results will be good. However, the very commitment to one developmental route means that the firm (or the economy) is wide open to unpleasant surprises from other directions. Then even good results on its chosen path just might not be good enough.

Complete knowledge, which is what conventional economics assumes, means the absence of uncertainty. So there's no need to internalize the risk. Nor would there be any genuine rivalry. Instead, there would merely be a market equilibrium that was already the best of all possible worlds.

Ironically, it is only the cartel in a stagnant industry that approximates this model of classic "competition." Yet this is hardly surprising. Keynes was British, and drew his material from the experience of British industry in the 1920s and '30s, which by then was organized into cartels amidst industrial stagnation.

Only a truly competitive firm, or economy, will sincerely act on the principle of uncertainty, by internalizing risk. Such a firm, or economy, does not act as though it already has all the answers. It does not believe that it already knows what the future will be.

What results, says Klein, is "predictable unpredictability." We can be confident that things won't stay the same, but we don't know which things will change nor how they will change.

Different firms try to find ways that things might change, and to work on advancing such changes as will be to their own advantage. Klein explains:

Because firms cannot predict each other's discoveries, they undertake different approaches toward achieving the same goal. And because not all of the approaches will turn out to be equally successful, the pursuit of parallel paths provides the options required for smooth progress. On the other hand, the rate of advance in an industry will depend on the rate of competitive interaction.

This statement has two further implications. First, the more firms there are in an industry, the more likely there will be competition. Second, the higher the level of uncertainty in a given industry, the more likely there will be a wide variety of approaches to improving productivity.

The high-technology industry does have a high level of uncertainty. However, in Texas, there are only a handful of research and development consortia engaged in high-tech efforts. And, as mentioned, high-tech is a very small part of our present and future employment, both nationally and in Texas.

Yet there are thousands of firms in Texas alone that provide products and services that use relatively low technology. And the overwhelming majority of these firms are small.

Klein says that firms which are successful innovators do more than just internalize risk. They are also very open to what he called "hints from the environment." They are "receptive to negative feedback."

Small firms tend to have an advantage here, because even the highest management of a small firm is still much involved with outsiders: customers and suppliers. Top management in these firms also tends to be involved in workplace activities at the lowest level.

One of Klein's major discoveries was the role of subcontractors in conceiving and developing many of the technological breakthroughs his book discusses. This lends credence to Jacobs's discussion of the export multiplier.

Local independent firms that act as suppliers to larger firms have many other customers using the same or similar products. Some of these customers are other manufacturers. Some of them are end-users. So, in supplying these larger firms, the local independent firm is exposed to a wide variety of information about the market, about the various uses of its products, and about possible improvements to it.

The local independent firm always has the incentive to make improvements in its products that will yield further revenues and profits. It also has the incentive to make improvements in its own capital equipment, to further boost productivity. And because its range of products or services is relatively small, it can pay more attention to each of them. This increases the prospect of a worthwhile discovery even more.

It should come as no surprise that subcontractors play a very large role in Japanese manufactures.

Ries and Trout, in *Bottom-Up Marketing*, assert that large firms are at a disadvantage:

> One problem is the number of management layers between top and bottom. The more layers, the more you are insulated from the market.

Elsewhere in the book, they comment:

> Small companies are mentally closer to the front than big companies.

This is not to argue that large firms are incapable of innovation. There are too many examples to the contrary. But, as chapter 8's description of large firms indicated, the very scale of operations in most large firms, and the geographical isolation of functions from one another, tend to work against innovation.

Ries and Trout quote T.K. Quinn, a former chairman of General Electric Credit Corporation:

> Not a single distinctively new home appliance has ever been created by one of the giant concerns—not the first washing machine, electric range, dryer, iron or ironer, electric lamp, refrigerator, toaster, fan, heating pad, razor, lawn mower, freezer, air conditioner, vacuum cleaner, dishwasher, or grill.

With regard to high technology, things may be different today. Perhaps the best way to achieve breakthroughs here is to organize a Manhattan Project consortium such as MCC or Sematech. Whether or not this is so is not the immediate concern of this book. But it seems obvious that no one would argue the case for organizing research and development consortia to create the mundane sort of products on Quinn's list.

Yet the firms that make the future equivalent of these humdrum manufactures are the firms that will probably prove the greatest sources of future employment, import replacements, and export multipliers—in short, of economic development. And since the large firms, in general, aren't interested in such low-tech endeavors, we ought to find ways to assist small firms in making this effort.

Klein's *Dynamic Economics* presented his study of the history of three American industries: aircraft, autos, and semiconductors. What he found is that all too often, after the fact, corporate historians claimed that crucial innovations were the result of some grand strategy on the part of top management.

In reality, though, Klein discovered that the crucial innovations did not result from top management alone, although it of course was involved. Klein concluded that what he called "risk internalization," "openness to hints from the environment," and "receptivity to negative feedback" were the crucial factors.

As he commented about the aircraft industry:

> No doubt, when business school experts on business strategy explain Boeing's huge success in the field of commercial jets, the story will be something like this: the adoption of a brilliant strategy to diversify into the jet field, in which the sale of bombers to the military was to be closely followed by the penetration of the commercial market, and the adoption of detailed and thorough tactical plans to implement this strategy. If you believe the top management's job is to make strategic plans, and the middle management's job is to assure the plans are carried out, how else can Boeing's success be explained?

Of course, this is precisely what corporate America thinks the respective roles of top management and middle management are. This is why so many firms have departments for strategic planning, often composed entirely of lawyers and MBA financial analysts: People who've never even seen the inside of a factory, never had to sell to a customer, and never had to negotiate with a supplier.

If it should happen that the course a firm takes does prove successful, then naturally top management takes the credit, congratulating itself on the brilliance of its "strategic planning." In government, this sort of thing happens all the time, where politicians scramble to take the credit for successes that often resulted from pure happenstance. Within a corporation (or government), who is going to challenge top management's misplaced pride, and thus risk losing his or her job?

Klein continues:

> But my understanding, from interviewing people who were actually involved, is that Boeing's success in the field of commercial jets resulted not so much from brilliant planning as it did from the necessity to survive in a highly uncertain environment and from the ability to turn misfortunes into opportunities.

In short, Boeing took it one step at a time. And because top management hadn't decided in advance exactly what they were looking for, they were quite open to a variety of alternatives.

This does not mean that we should return to seat-of-the-pants management. However, contemporary managers—and contemporary advocates of economic policy—have gone too far toward the opposite extreme. There is today a quest for certainty, carrying Peter Drucker's famous "management by objectives" to absurd lengths. And, once a project is underway, the attitude seems to be: "Don't confuse me with the facts. My mind's made up."

The Serendipity Factor

The concept of risk implies far more than a willingness to take a chance. It implies acceptance of uncertainty as to the means. This relates to what might be called the "serendipity factor." The discussion in Klein's and Jacobs's works point to this as a vital element in economic success.

For example, Jacobs traces the early history of the 3M Corporation, formerly known as Minnesota Mining and Manufacturing. In 1902 that firm consisted merely of two owners and several manual laborers, who were "engaged in digging, crushing, sorting, and selling sand" to manufacturers of metal products in Minneapolis who used the sand as an abrasive.

The proprietors realized that they could also use sand to make sandpaper, for carpenters and others who worked in wood. The two men did not invent sandpaper. They just wanted to enter that market.

To do so, they began to develop their own adhesive, in-house. But they weren't able to come up with anything that was good enough to compete with the sandpaper already on the market. Their adhesive was good enough to make masking tape, though, which they sold to housepainters. They went on to develop other tapes, of which the best-known is Scotch brand cellophane tape.

Today, of course, 3M offers a vast array of tapes, including high-tech magnetic tape. 3M also, eventually, found an adhesive that enabled it to produce competitive sandpaper. And 3M's adhesive for pipe-coating holds the major share of that market. The company's most innovative recent product for the consumer market uses an adhesive for the "Post-it" message pads found in virtually every office and in a lot of homes.

This pattern in 3M's history illustrates what Jacobs calls "adding new work to old." With the benefit of hindsight, we can see that each new 3M product was a logical outgrowth of its previous work. But the most important point is that 3M took it one step at a time. There was no grand strategy at work, whereby the original two owners decided to diversify into the adhesives industry. And, as we've seen, their first effort at diversification failed.

In the story of the Sony Corporation, by contrast, its role in consumer electronics represented a complete break with its past. Sony also was started by just two men. But their original intention was to be a firm that manufactured electric rice-cookers. Unfortunately—at least in the short run—they weren't any good at that, and they nearly went bankrupt. As a desperate measure to generate income, they started repairing radios. The rest is history.

Klein implies, and Jacobs explicitly asserts, that the process of adding new work to old is usually governed by what's called here the serendipity factor. Jacobs explains:

> The point is that when new work is added to older work, the

addition often cuts ruthlessly across categories of work, no matter how one may analyze the categories. Only in stagnant economies does work stay docilely within given categories. And wherever it is forced to stay within prearranged categories—whether by zoning, by economic planning, or by guilds, associations or unions—the process of adding new work to old can occur little if at all.

Jacobs's export multiplier and import-replacement multiplier are clearly the prime sources of what she calls "new work." A healthy economy will be constantly adding new work, illustrating what Klein calls "predictable unpredictability." Yet their empirical research indicates that this is not something that can be planned, in advance, from the top down. It is, instead, a bottom-up phenomenon.

Klein asserts that another crucial factor in enhancing innovation is a tolerance for ambiguity. The smaller firm has fewer layers of management. Top management will be much closer to the research and development, and in fact the R&D will be much more informal. This means that people don't have their egos on the line. They aren't protecting bureaucratic turf and departmental budgets. And the people who are tinkering with a potential innovation don't have a distant superior monitoring formal reports that calculate the return-on-investment to date.

Because the people involved have so much less to lose, whether of money or status, they can afford to take bigger risks. They also can afford to take a "wait and see" attitude. Klein comments:

> What limits the dynamic capability of large structured organizations, whether in the automobile industry or in the Defense Department? The basic problem with such organizations is that, while they can be programmed to say "yes" or "no," they cannot be programmed to say "maybe."

Decisive executives pride themselves on being able to quickly evaluate alternatives, to give a "yes" or "no" and then get on with the program. This attitude may well be appropriate after an innovation has been achieved. Then the only questions concern the method of production, the means of distribution, and the advertising approach. But at the R&D stage, such decisiveness is counterproductive.

In 1970, Arthur B. Bronwell, dean of engineering at the University of Connecticut, edited a book called *Science and Technology in the World of the Future*. One of his own essays in that volume was entitled "The Creative Society." In it, he discussed at length the careers of architect Frank Lloyd Wright and scientist Robert Goddard.

Both men were heavily involved in creating new technologies—the one in building design, the other in rocketry. Both were what Bronwell called "enemies of the conventionally wise" and so both were reviled by the conventionally wise.

Wright's contributions to our world are well-known; Goddard's, less so. Said Bronwell: "Goddard made every major discovery of modern rockets with the exception of the electronic guidance systems, which grew out of later technologies."

In analyzing the careers of these two men, and others like them, Bronwell noted:

> New ideas are often tenuous and amorphic. No matter how important they might ultimately prove to be, in the embryo stages they are fragile and can easily get lost in the sea of doubts, confusions, and uncertainties. There is little that can be proved; hence their ideas make only a feeble imprint before the terra firma meetings of the learned societies. Their future potentials may be all wrapped up in the philosophical realms of thought that do not easily tie down to the existing world of reality.

The quest for instant certainty inherent in the top-down approach to economic revival in Texas is, above all, an intolerance for the very uncertainties Bronwell refers to.

Our present efforts at economic development are highly inefficient, at best, and perhaps even counter-productive. This is because they result from the macroeconomic approach, outlined in chapter 4. Granted, if the only alternative were microeconomics, we'd have no choice but to continue this way. However, mesoeconomics, "bootstrap economics," gives us both the theory and the practice that will enable us to transcend the either/or limitations of the conventional wisdom.

We don't need to gamble our economic future on the predictions of a handful of self-proclaimed experts and their followers. We can safely trust ourselves.

Most of those who dominate economic policy-making in Texas come from large bureaucratic organizations. They carry with them the habits of mind which prevail in those organizations. That is why they have such a preference for large-scale, top-down, "magic wand" solutions based on grand strategy and predicting the future.

We would do much better to opt for predictable unpredictability which, in the long run, will probably be far more productive. Chapter 11 ("Entropy vs. Energy") discusses specific ways to do this. But first we need to take a closer look at so-called "industrial policy."

10 | Industrial Policy vs. Bootstrap Economics

What we need, and have lacked, is the ability to target our incentives to those who can make good use of them without wasting taxpayers' money on those who cannot.

—David L. Birch
"The Job Generation Process"

The term "industrial policy" is seldom used, approvingly, in Texas. This is because of its association with certain liberals (or "neoliberals") in Cambridge, Massachusetts. Instead, Texans who favor industrial policy usually talk in terms of "a master plan for economic development." Today the model is post-war Japan, but the idea has been around for a long, long time.

Its earlier vogue in the 20th century was roughly three generations ago. Victor Schoffelmayer wrote a book on the Texas economy in 1935, just before the Texas centennial, called *Texas at the Crossroads*. In it, he said:

> Texas agriculture and industry, as partners in the years to come, should have the benefit of a plan of action looking to the widest development of the State's resources and the setting up of enterprises at strategic locations and with every likelihood of success. A planning body, on which technicians and practical business men will serve their State in mapping a plan of attack, could make an important contribution to the progress of Texas. There are various districts now in existence from which materials could be drawn toward a compact central agency ... The time for wise planning and coordinated action for the good of the entire State has arrived.

Those words could have been written today. Variations of those remarks have become part of the conventional wisdom of our economic and political leaders in recent years. The problem with this approach becomes obvious when we see Schoffelmayer's comments that immediately follow those just excerpted:

> Italy, that amazing land of art and beauty, again is in the midst of a Renaissance. Not painters, sculptors, architects, poets, and papal geniuses, however, are responsible for this remarkable rebirth, but hard-headed economic planners carried forward by the force of an iron-willed leader—Mussolini.

Ahem.

Industrial policy has been regarded correctly as quasi-socialistic thinking. Both liberals and conservatives have associated socialism with left-wing politics. Accordingly, liberals have favored socialist policies but, being Americans, they use terms such as "New Deal" or "The Great Society." Conservatives have denounced socialist policies—but only with respect to the poor. When it comes to the rich (whether big business or big banks), conservatives, too, endorse socialist policies but again under different names, such as "federal loan guarantees" for failing corporations, or "marketing orders" in agribusiness.

Both liberals and conservatives forget that socialism can be right-wing as well as left-wing, as the example of Mussolini shows. Indeed, the word "Nazi" is just the verbal contraction of the German words for "national socialist." Conservative socialism is known as fascism.

Any discussion of socialism immediately gets charged with emotion. But the essence of socialism, whether right-wing or left-wing, is an effort to avoid risk-taking on the part of its beneficiaries. This process has long been at work in America, too, with the quasi-socialist policies, both left-wing and right-wing, of our political parties. As Klein noted:

> ... [T]he main difference between the two great political parties is that whereas one is concerned with exempting big corporations and wealthy individuals from risk-taking, the other is concerned with insuring that the common man will not have to engage in

risk-taking. In short, the goal of American politics is a society of politicians in which no one need use his imagination.

While Klein is correct in defining the hidden similarity between the two major parties, he is unfair in accusing politicians of a lack of imagination. Our politicians have proven themselves very imaginative in finding new ways to reduce risk-taking in America—and to do it in the name of restoring American competitiveness! This trick takes a great deal of imaginative rhetoric and obfuscation.

David Stockman's book, *The Triumph of Politics*, is an eye-opening case study of how the system works. Given his background as a divinity student, it's not surprising that he ends his book with a round of mea culpa, condemning himself as a foolish sinner. He would have done better to have studied Greek mythology in school, for he then would have realized that he is a modern Cassandra. He too has the power of prophecy, but then also has the curse of not having his prophecies believed before it's too late. His analysis was accurate. And sometime, in retrospect, we'll acknowledge this.

The discussion here is not to argue the case for laissez faire, the way the libertarians do. Their hypothetical system never existed, despite their claims to the contrary. Nor would it last long in practice today—even if such a system were desirable, which it definitely is not.

For example, the Libertarian Party (although not all libertarians) seeks to abolish the CIA, the FBI, and all public schools, among other things. Further, if the American people want national defense, they should contract to hire various corporations to provide private armies, navies, and air forces—a return to the condottieri of the Renaissance. (On the other hand, their proposal to abolish the IRS sounds pretty good!)

Laissez faire is not the solution to our problems. However, it is also clear that the "lazy fare" we have now, for rich and poor alike, is also not the solution to our problems—and in fact makes our problems much worse.

What's happening in our economy is something very much like cancer. Cancer is abnormal growth of cells, growth that feeds on the rest of the body and which can eventually kill it.

The growth of vested interests is also cancerous. Their representatives insist that if their industry isn't saved by government intervention, then they will suffer terribly—and the rest of us will then suffer too, by extension. Using arguments that rely more on emotion than reason, representatives for the special interests convince us to divert resources from more productive uses, to help them merely to survive.

Then, having survived one round by partially cannibalizing the rest of our economy, the cancer of vested interest continues to grow until it again has problems of its own making. The best current example of this process is the bailout of the savings and loan industry. This will eventually cost vastly more than the officially projected figure.

Mancur Olson, an economist at the University of Maryland and a former president of the Southern Economics Association, did a study of this. His book on it, published in 1982, is called *The Rise and Decline of Nations: Economic Growth, Stagflation, and Social Rigidities.* (This should not be confused with *The Rise and Fall of the Great Powers,* a more recent work by Paul Kennedy which will be discussed in chapter 12.) Instead of using the loaded term "vested interests," Olson made up a neutral term, "distributional coalitions." He describes them as follows:

> To achieve their objectives, distributional coalitions must use their lobbying power to influence governmental policy or their collusive power to influence the market. These two influences affect not only efficiency, economic growth, and exclusion of entrants in a society, but also the relative importance of different institutions and activities. Lobbying increases the complexity of regulation and the scope of government ... An increase in the payoffs from lobbying and cartel activity, as compared with the payoffs from production, means more resources are devoted to politics and cartel activity and fewer resources are devoted to production.

The bureaucracies of the vested interests (or distributional coalitions) become quite smug. They believe—often correctly—that the market will conform to the needs of the firms, and unions, and the government officials concerned with that industry. So they refuse to reform to meet the needs of the market. They accept no risk. They're impervious to meaningful feedback, especially negative feedback, from the economic environment.

As the vested interests consume more and more of the healthy economic resources, they guarantee that when disaster strikes—and it will strike—the disaster will be much more widespread than if we had successfully contained their diseased behavior in as small a range of operation as possible.

What makes the situation tragic, though, is that unlike cancer in the human body, economic cancer is a normal occurrence. This is where Olson makes his most original contribution. The longer an economy enjoys uninterrupted political continuity, he says, the more vested interests will build up and interlock with "the powers that be" in the political system.

Over the years, mutual understandings build up. The protegees of government officials routinely interact with the protegees of corporate, labor, and academic officials at an early stage in their careers. This reinforces the implicit attitude of "You scratch my back and I'll scratch yours."

This interaction is so extensive that it resembles a baseball diamond, with the players moving from one base to another: industry, government, academia, and consulting or law firms. The back-scratching occurs automatically, in the name of "consensus-building."

The ultimate result, in a system that's supposedly capitalist, is "industrial policy." Industrial policy is the bureaucrat's heaven on earth. Small wonder that so many academicians, who come from one of the most stultifying bureaucratic environments of all, should endorse it so enthusiastically.

And of course industrial policy is also the (incumbent) politician's dream. Vested interests have the surplus funds to hire functionaries who can interface with the government bureaucracy—and with elected officials. The vested interests also have the surplus funds to make handsome campaign contributions in return for services rendered, or to be rendered. It's an old story. As Olson comments:

> Congressmen and Senators can gain exceptional support by helping constituents to obtain particular services or exceptions from government ... For this reason ... legislators seek more bureaucratic or manipulable legislation that further increases the

importance of the constituent services that help them to be re-elected.

And if we're really honest with ourselves, we'll admit that we all like the thought of being able to call up a member of Congress or a U.S. senator, to speak with a top aide to request a special favor, and to know that the favor will be granted. It's much easier and more enjoyable to solve problems by picking up a phone and using personal connections to "fix" something, instead of doing the hard thinking and the hard work that goes with really trying to solve a problem on our own.

Thus our elected officials, especially in Washington but also in Austin, have a vested interest in promoting the economic cancer that's eating away at our future. But it's our own laziness, and fear, and greed, and vanity, that enables them, even encourages them, to survive politically by helping the rest of us to become cancer cells in our own small way—which, after all, is what this amounts to.

The ultimate example of bureaucratic cancer in a free society is Britain, according to Olson:

> The logic of the argument implies that countries that have had democratic freedom of organization without upheaval or invasion the longest will suffer the most from growth-repressing organizations and combinations. This helps to explain why Great Britain, the major nation with the longest immunity from dictatorship, invasion, or revolution, has had in this century a lower rate of growth than other large, developed democracies.
>
> Britain has precisely the powerful network of special-interest organizations that the argument developed here would lead us to expect in a country with its record of military security and democratic stability. The number and power of its trade unions need no description.

And it isn't just the power of the trade unions, either. Does the United States have "the British disease"? The answer is obvious.

Olson's work does not try to provide a simplistic one-factor explanation for all the phenomena discussed in his book, *The Rise and Decline of Nations: Economic Growth, Stagflation, and Social Rigidities.* The excerpts and capsulations presented here are just highlights of his thorough and scholarly analysis.

But the implications of his work for the United States are distressing. If we do not have the courage and the will to renounce our own desires for "cancer economics" then, he says:

> The incentive to produce is diminished; the incentive to seek a larger share of what is produced increases. The reward for pleasing those to whom we sell our goods or labor declines, while the reward for evading or exploiting regulations, politics, and bureaucracy ... becomes greater. These changes in the patterns of incentives in turn deflect the direction of a society's evolution.

The direction of our society's evolution has been clear for some time now. The sort of "games" Olson describes above are nothing new, of course. But they never before had society's approval as the norm, as praiseworthy behavior. Previously, such dubious activity always occurred on the sly. When exposed, it was condemned. Today, in contrast, we make heroes of the very executives whose skills are merely those of manipulation, not creation.

This is truly amazing. On the one hand, we condemn as "robber barons" the giants of the 19th century who built up all the great industries which have been the mainstay of our economy throughout the 20th century. On the other hand, we champion as "geniuses" the B.S. artists who are deconstructing our economy, driving corporations into the ground, and making entire industries prey to foreign conquest—all because these people have a knack for making tons of money at it.

However, even those who condemn the corporate "greenmailers" and the leveraged-buyout artists still approve of the alleged trend toward a "services economy"—chief of which are the financial services. This has been endorsed as "progress" by those who ought to know better. It has attained intellectual respectability as "the post-industrial society."

However, America is producing fewer and fewer goods. More and more, we are merely selling goods made in other countries. Often, a label that says "American made" only means that the final assembly, or the distribution, is by Americans. Even much of our military hardware contains a significant percentage of foreign components. This means that eventually we will need our suppliers more than they will need us, because they will have the technology for creating and maintaining the hardware that's absolutely essential for our economy and society.

What Olson called "the incentive to produce" certainly has been diminished, by regulations, politics, and bureaucracy. In the wonderful service economy that allegedly awaits us, we can perhaps make a living taking in each others' laundry. The washing machines and the clothes themselves will be manufactured in other nations.

Even more ominous, perhaps, is that foreign rivals who now dominate our manufacturing sector have begun to encroach on the services sector with great success. "Goods" and "services" aren't two mutually-exclusive realms. As Jane Jacobs showed in her book of economic history, *The Economy of Cities*, goods and services are complementary and interdependent. Those Americans who gladly "kissed off" our smokestack industries are in for some very unpleasant surprises.

The Economic Darwinists
Of course, the champions of industrial policy deny that this discussion has anything to do with them. In fact, they have revived the 19th-century doctrine of Social Darwinism and talk in terms of "survival of the fittest." A century ago that doctrine was used to justify the ruthless business practices of the corporate empire-builders, and to deny sympathy to society's "losers." The new Economic Darwinists, instead, see their theory in what they would call humanitarian terms.

The idea is that designated "sunset" industries are doomed. Permitting them to survive would merely delay the inevitable and prolong the eventual agony. In the meantime, these industries will be virtually wasting resources that could be put to better use. So one aspect of industrial policy is to perform economic euthanasia: corporate "mercy killing." The victims' assets will then be transferred to more promising "sunrise" industries.

In its own way, however, this approach is even more ruthless than that of 19th-century Social Darwinism. Back then, people and companies at least had a chance to fight back. In doing so, they might survive instead of succumbing. But with industrial policy, those marked for death have no recourse. This is done in the name of economic evolution. The government will get to define "the fittest," which in turn will determine who gets to survive.

If Jacobs, Klein, Olson, Ries, and Trout are correct, however, industrial policy is the worst possible thing we could do in this country—and in Texas. Industrial policy is based on a bogus "certainty," on "predicting the future," and on the "megatrends" approach. It completely disregards internationalization of risk, openness to hints from the environment, receptivity to negative feedback, "predictable unpredictability," and the "serendipity factor." And if the corporate histories presented by Klein and Jacobs are accurate, industrial policy completely ignores the lessons of those histories.

Would-be makers of industrial policy point to the success of Japan, and claim that industrial policy is the cause. Yet they always omit two crucial points.

First, Japan's industrial policy started in the late 19th century. It was consciously modeled on that of France and Germany. All three were oriented toward war-making potential. So was the Soviet Union's industrial policy, after the 1917 communist coup. In all these countries, a war-oriented industrial policy succeeded, more or less. But in the postwar era, only Japan has been successful with industrial policy in terms of peacetime economics. Everywhere else it has failed. This strongly suggests that industrial policy in itself is not the key to success.

Second, the nature of the Japanese economy is quite different from that of the American economy. Industrial policy has indeed worked well in Japan. But for it to succeed in America, we would have to virtually remake our entire system of economic organization, our financial institutions, and even our political system.

One major factor in Japan's industrial policy is the power and prestige of the government bureaucracy. In America, the "best and brightest" head for the top law schools and business schools. Then they enter the private sector and make their fortunes. In Japan, the graduates of the top schools do not pursue post-graduate education. They go straight into the Ministry of Finance and the Ministry of International Trade and Industry. And they stay there for the rest of their careers.

Granted, a lot of civil service employees of the American federal government also spend their careers on the public payroll. But they don't have the prestige or respect that Japan's civil servants have—in part because Americans know that employees of the federal government usually aren't the cream of the crop.

What's more, the best and brightest among Japan's civil servants eventually rise to the top of their ministries, and are truly in control of what happens. In America, even the best civil servants are faced with a "ceiling." They know that the several layers above that ceiling will be composed of political appointees: under-secretary of this, assistant secretary of that, deputy under-assistant of whatever. And even though American career civil servants do have a lot of power, that power is negative: the subtle power to frustrate the will of their political-appointee superiors.

Further, in America there is enormous interference by politicians and political appointees in the activities of the civil service. This is the notorious practice of "micro-management." In Japan, this simply doesn't happen. Whether or not the one is good and the other is bad is irrelevant to this discussion. The important fact is that it is a fundamentally different system.

The American political appointees, frankly, are often hacks. They get their jobs not because they are qualified for them, but because they are protegees of a powerful politician. They can use their political-appointee job as a credential when seeking elective office or a high-paying consulting job later on.

Sometimes the appointees are not political protegees, but instead are watchdogs for a special-interest group. This is notoriously the practice even with respect to some cabinet positions. In such cases, the appointee's agenda is not that of working for the common good. Rather, he or she works for the advancement of the special-interest group, often at the expense of the common good.

But whether the political appointees are noble or base, effective or ineffective, is ultimately almost irrelevant. Given the nature of our political system, the appointees are seldom in office for more than a few years. They have little opportunity for long-term project development. And, since the appointees usually come in with no prior experience in the department in question, they must first take a long time to build up the working relationships necessary to achieve anything.

Just about the time they're in a position to be able to really do something, they decide to leave for greener pastures. Either that, or there's a change in administration, and the new president replaces the old appointees with a new team of his own choosing, to head in a different direction.

This brings us to another factor in the success of Japan's industrial policy: Japan is a one-party polity. The Liberal Democratic Party has been in power there for nearly forty years. The top elected officials in that party normally rotate through all the top ministries as titular heads. The real boss of each ministry is the vice minister, a career civil servant. The official boss, the minister, has little to do with the workings of the department. The title is merely a prestige symbol, a sign that this is one of the most important people in the Liberal Democratic Party. The American system doesn't work this way at all. Not only do we have two major parties, they even lack the unity and cohesiveness of the party system in Britain.

Further, Japan's economy is extremely concentrated. When we look at the success of Sony in consumer electronics, for example, we think we're looking just at Sony. But Sony is a member of the Mitsui cartel. Most of Japan's economic activity is in the hands of a handful of cartels that dominate every industry. Just as General Motors, for example, can use money from one division (such as Chevrolet) to finance activities in other divisions (such as Electronic Data Systems or the diesel-locomotive manufacturing division), so the members of Japan's various cartels tacitly work together—but on a vastly larger scale.

Japanese corporations are able to take the long view because they are backed up by the enormously deep pockets of the cartels to which they belong. Eventually these, in turn, are backed up by the even deeper pockets of the Japanese government—through its various state banks that make the Federal Reserve look like a local bank out in the boondocks.

American corporations are financed by stock offerings and debt securities. Institutional investors are the main source of funds to buy these financial instruments. Institutional investors work on behalf of their own clients—and their clients demand a good return on their money. If a given corporation's performance doesn't meet the target rate of return, the institutional investors won't fund them. This is precisely why American corporations must take a short-term approach.

Japanese corporations don't have to go to the public for their capital. Japan does have stock and bond markets for publicly traded issues, of course. However, only a small fraction of Japan's corporate securities are held by the general public or by institutional investors who represent the general public.

Most of Japan's corporate securities are held by other corporations that belong to the same cartel as the issuing firm. And they don't look at these investments as a source of income or capital gains through appreciation of share value. They look at these funds in the same way that General Motors looks at a $100 million loan from Cadillac to Buick. It's for the good of the whole, in the long run.

If Mitsui Busan, the huge trading company that handles exports and imports for the Mitsui cartel, wants a billion dollars, for example, each of the companies in the Mitsui cartel chips in an amount based on its size and strength. Mitsui Busan, in turn, is expected to contribute to the needs of other firms in the Mitsui cartel. This portfolio approach to financing enormously reduces the risk to any one firm for any one loan it has extended, because the risk is spread out over all the members of the cartel.

The unique nature of Japan's corporate financing enables firms to get long-term capital at a low cost. This gives each firm a significant advantage in the market. American firms simply can't afford to sell at cost or at a loss, for long. Japanese firms can, and do, in order to build up market share. They know that once they've driven their weaker (foreign) competitors out of the market, they can raise prices and recoup their original investment.

The government side of Japan's industrial policy plays second fiddle to the corporate side. True, the two work closely together, forming what we often call "Japan, Inc." But it's the unique nature of Japan's cartel system that is the key ingredient in the success of Japan's industrial policy.

The cartels the West has known have almost always consisted just of firms in one industry. It has been extremely rare to have one firm, or one conglomerate, belong to a cartel that dominated more than one industry. Earlier in this century, DuPont owned General Motors, but that's the closest we've come in the United States.

Imagine if roughly 80 percent of the American economy were controlled by just six super-conglomerates. One of them would consist of McDonnell-Douglas Aircraft, Ford Motor Company, Dow Chemical, General Electric (which in turn owns RCA and NBC), the Union Pacific Railroad, Continental Airlines, IBM, Citibank, and about 100 other companies. A second super-conglomerate might own Boeing Aircraft Corporation, General Motors, the Burlington Northern Railroad, DuPont, Lykes Shipping, American Airlines, Honeywell, Chase Manhattan Bank, and maybe another 150 companies. That is what the situation is like in Japan, and what any given American firm, in any given industry, is up against.

If the American economy were organized this way, and if the federal government actually encouraged the cartel members in each industry to work together, and if organized labor were virtually powerless (as it is in Japan), and if Wall Street shrank to insignificance, and if the American people didn't mind all this, then industrial policy on the Japanese model might work here. Otherwise, we had better think of something else.

One suggestion has been to shovel federal dollars out to corporations doing research and development. Indeed, that's a big source of Sematech's funding—but Sematech is a Defense Department project, not an effort to produce superior commercial goods.

The problem with using federal money to fund corporations directly (versus consortia) is that there simply are too many potential candidates for funding in America. The Japanese don't have this problem, because of the aforementioned cartels.

But even if there were only a handful of candidates in America (as is the situation with high-definition TV, for example), there's another problem: The worst that can happen to American corporations that waste such money would be that they wouldn't get any more federal money. It doesn't work that way in Japan. If the other members of the cartel—or especially the Japanese government—have put big bucks into a high priority R&D project, and the effort isn't succeeding, heads will roll.

We simply don't have a good method of selecting the right candidates for our funding, nor do we have a good method of enforcing a judicious use of public money. And so, too often, political connections determine the result. We need only look at how our defense contractors have wasted so much of the R&D money they got, when they were supposed to be working to enhance our national security, to realize that commercial R&D would probably fare no better if funded by the federal government.

This new form of Social Darwinism, "Economic Darwinism," that advocates industrial policy is, as mentioned, based on "the survival of the fittest." When the original doctrine of Social Darwinism was first formulated in the 19th century, T.H. Huxley took issue with it. He said we should use a different approach, such that "its influence is directed, not so much to the survival of the fittest, as to the fitting of as many as possible to survive."

Assuming that Klein, Jacobs, and Olson are correct, then Huxley's interpretation should be the one we use to guide our economic policies for the future of Texas. David Birch's study, already mentioned, further supports this.

Birch analyzed the data on 5.6 million American businesses nationwide, over a seven-year time series. He examined the data first for 1969, then again for 1972, 1974, and 1976. He checked the location of each business each time, and the number of employees at each firm.

Birch continued his research after the publication of his first report in 1979. By 1986, he had studied 12 million firms. His 1987 book, *Job Creation in America*, confirmed and updated his earlier findings.

In his 1979 report, "The Job Generation Process," Birch had made a common-sense list of the six ways that employment levels can change:

1. through the birth of a new firm,
2. through the death of an existing firm,
3. through the expansion of a firm,
4. through the contraction of a firm,
5. from the move into a local economy by a firm previously

located elsewhere, or
6. from the move out of a local economy by a firm that had been located there.

Birch's studies indicate that job loss from the death or contraction of existing firms in any given year is high: 8 percent. Surprisingly, this rate was virtually constant throughout the years of his surveys, and held for all regions of the country.

So just to hold the level of employment constant, a local economy must replace 8 percent of its jobs each year. For employment to show a net increase, then, a local economy must develop enough to be able to generate more than an 8 percent job growth each year. When we hear, for example, that Texas unemployment has risen by 4 percent, what this really means is that job replacement has fallen by 4 percent. In other words, we only created half the new jobs that we needed to create just to hold our own.

Current economic-development efforts concentrate on large firms. The most common activity is public relations designed to get large firms to relocate into the local economy. But of the six ways that employment can grow in a local economy, Birch said that the least important is business relocation:

> Virtually no firms migrate from one area to another in the sense of hiring a moving van and relocating their operations. The oft-cited move of textiles and shoes from New England to the South represented a rare fluke in the 1950s, not an example of a significant process today.

That statement is from his 1979 report. In his 1987 book, Birch expanded that conclusion:

> The fact of the matter is that however highly publicized they may be, relocated firms are insignificant from a job creation or loss standpoint. Many firms move each year, but the vast majority do so comparatively short distances, and virtually all—like IBM and Union Carbide—within the same metropolitan area. Most relocations out of New York, Philadelphia, and Washington (all of which are experiencing significant outmoves) are to nearby places—New Jersey, Connecticut, Virginia, or Maryland ... The firms will go a handful of miles to Long Island, not to Montana ...

Political leaders who fall over themselves seeking relocations are like shoppers going into a grocery store to purchase apples, when it might be wiser to plant a few apple trees and wait until they bear fruit. Of course, this is a long-term investment; but the sooner they start, the faster will the fruits be harvested.

As *Job Creation in America* makes clear, Birch's findings are even more conclusive now than they were in 1979. Yet nearly all of our economic "development" organizations concentrate their efforts on corporate relocations. Throughout the country, 15,000 groups are doing exactly the same thing. The State of Texas even runs a training program for local officials, complete with the issuance of a certificate to graduates declaring that they are now "experts" in the art of wooing out-of-state firms to Texas (at least in theory).

These efforts are understandable, insofar as it's easy to determine a cause-and-effect relationship between one's efforts and the results. Success here is obvious and very gratifying: There are interviews on television, ribbon-cutting ceremonies, and junkets to exotic places to solicit still more relocations.

Efforts that succeed in preserving existing jobs are less obvious, except in dramatic cases where employees do a leveraged buyout of a firm that would otherwise go out of business, or where political pressure is brought to bear to keep a government facility open.

Birch offers more reasons why it's a big mistake to concentrate on large firms with respect to job generation. For the United States as a whole, according to Birch:
1. Small firms (those with 20 or fewer employees) generated 66% of all new jobs generated in the U.S.
2. Small, independent firms [a subgroup of the one above] generated 52% of the total.
3. Middle sized and large firms, on balance, provided relatively few new jobs.
4. There was considerable regional variation in this pattern. Small businesses generated all net new jobs in the Northeast . . . and 54% and 60% in the South and West, respectively.

Birch did say that branch plants contributed significantly to job generation. However, as the illustrations in chapter 8 showed, branch plants can prove counterproductive in the long run, even when they remain active. Further, as many Texas communities have learned to their chagrin, what a distant corporate headquarters giveth, it can also taketh away—often without warning.

To look more closely at Birch's findings, we see that they further confirm the role of Jacobs's export multiplier and import replacement multiplier, with their reliance on independent local vendors:

1. Young firms play a crucial role, generating about 80% of all replacement jobs.
2. This pattern holds across all sectors of the economy and across all regions.

Granted, this flatly contradicts statistics issued by the U.S. Small Business Administration with respect to Texas for the period 1976-82. According to the SBA, for the six years mentioned, firms with 500 or more employees provided nearly 50 percent of all new jobs in Texas. Those with less than 20 employees created only about one-fourth of all new jobs.

The fact that the Texas SBA survey started in 1976, (the last year covered in Birch's original study), and ended six years later, might seem to indicate a change in the pattern Birch saw across the eight years of his initial research. But a more likely explanation is that the years from 1976 to 1982 were the peak of the "go go" years in the oil boom.

Birch published his original findings before the oil-business reversal. Yet he had already seen that what goes up must come down. His work indicated that firms and industries that had the fastest, biggest growth in boom times also had the fastest, biggest declines in a bust. His supplementary update, issued seven years after his first report, confirmed this:

> A big gain in the past tends also to lead to a higher than average expectation of a big loss. Volatility cuts both ways: what has gone up has a higher than average tendency to go down in the next period. The biggest gainers of all, curiously but very consistently, are establishments that declined most in the recent past, but survived. These establishments have a higher than average expectation of dying, but, if they make it, they are the ones *most*

likely to generate a large number of new jobs in the future. On balance, they are in fact three or four times more likely to be large job generators. (Emphasis added.)

The boom has long since ended in Texas. We now must deal with our situation in terms of the underlying long-term realities that Birch noted. And this is where his research becomes fascinating—and especially relevant to Texas. For the period covered by his initial study, he concluded:
1. The odds of an establishment dying over this 7-year period are quite high . . .
2. The odds of dying vs. contracting are quite sensitive to size—with a sharp break around 20 employees. Those establishments below 20 are more likely to die than contract. Those above 20 lay off part of their workforce before going out of business.
3. Of those who survive, *small* firms are four times more likely to expand than contract, and larger firms are 50 percent more likely to shrink than to grow. (Emphasis added.)

The obvious implication is that we should find a way to promote the survival of small existing firms, including new firms, and to support any expansion efforts they undertake.

Birch himself could not suggest ways to do this. In fact, he pointed out that "a massive bureaucracy would be required to monitor individual small businesses on the scale required to change the direction of an area's economy." He—quite rightly—opposed the expense involved, and feared the potential for favoritism:

> It is no wonder that efforts to stem the tide of job decline have been so frustrating—and largely unsuccessful. The firms that such efforts must reach are the most difficult to identify and the most difficult to work with. They tend to be independent. They are volatile. The very spirit that gives them their volatility and job generating powers is the same spirit that makes them unpromising partners for the development administrator.

> The easier strategy of working with larger, "known" corporations

whose behavior is better understood will not be, and has not been, very productive. Few of the net new jobs generated in our economy are generated by this group.

At that time, Birch had to rest content with stating the clear implication of his research:

> A pattern begins to emerge in all of this. The job generating firm tends to be small. It tends to be dynamic (or unstable, depending on your viewpoint)—the kind of firm that banks feel very uncomfortable about. It tends to be young. In short, the firms that can and do generate the most jobs are the ones that are the most difficult to reach through conventional policy initiatives.

Fortunately for Texas, and for the rest of America, some people in New Jersey and in Oregon came up with some unconventional policy initiatives that provide the essence of bootstrap economics. The next chapter presents their work.

11 | Entropy vs. Energy

> *We wanted a "bootstrap" approach that would be inexpensive and helpful to businesspeople like you who are already living, working and investing in Lane County. We wanted a program that would not be dependent upon the decisions of people outside Oregon. We wanted to build our economic development efforts around our best resource—local people.*
>
> —"Oregon Marketplace" Brochure

Scientists say that all systems, whether living or inanimate, tend to "run down." In fact, they say this entropy is inevitable. The universe itself, which supposedly started with a bang, will end with a whimper. Gradually, what had been well organized becomes chaos. Things fall apart.

Another way of describing entropy is to say that the amount of available energy will decrease. In a way this concept, first stated by physicists, is similar to the gradual decay we see in individual human beings, ending in death and the dissolution of the body.

The old domino player in White Oak, Texas, cited in chapter 2, expressed the attitude that entropy is inevitable in our economy: "We've had our day in the sun. Now, we're going to suffer, and there's nothing we can do about it." Such an attitude implies that even if we recover somewhat from our recent disaster, we will never again be an economic powerhouse.

Quite often in history, ideas from science are rephrased in terms of society. Social Darwinism, mentioned in the previous chapter, is one example. Marxism is another, modeled on the theory of electricity, which is why Marx called it "scientific socialism." For those who believe that entropy in the natural world must be reflected in the human portion of the natural world, the old domino player was right.

Yet for those who insist on thinking of society (and economics) in terms of science, there is cause for renewed optimism. Ilya Prigogine, a Belgian who served on the faculty at the University of Texas, made a momentous discovery for which he received the 1977 Nobel Prize in chemistry.

Prigogine showed that while, in the long run, the entire universe eventually will succumb to total entropy, in the short run there are systems that "run uphill" against the entropy.

These systems take in energy from the environment and organize it internally in such a way as to increase their own energy. They also "dump" their own entropy into the environment, adding to the disorder that's already there. So while the overall pattern is one of decline, individual systems can move toward greater complexity and power.

This scientific model seems apt for Texas today. The oil and agribusiness industries, which have been the foundation of our economy, have clearly had an enormous increase in their levels of entropy. Yet even within these industries, there are exceptions, moving uphill. Petrochemical refineries, for example, are enjoying another boom thanks to the low price of oil. And Texas agriculture also has some promising developments, described later in this chapter.

Even so, in the long run it's well-known that we must provide a new foundation for our future prosperity. What isn't so well known is that we never have been masters of our fate. (Chapter 5, "Money vs. Wealth," explained why.)

This chapter presents "bootstrap economics in a nutshell." Unlike the "grand strategy" approach that targets selected "sunrise" industries and writes off everything else, this mesoeconomic approach is based on predictable unpredictability.

Before proceeding to the real-life case studies that demonstrate the effectiveness of bootstrap economics in action, let's look at a well-intentioned Texas effort that went awry.

"Ivory Tower" Launches Lead Balloon
In the 1980s two academicians then at Southern Methodist University's Cox School of Business, Bernard Weinstein and Harold Gross, prepared "Target Industry Surveys" for various Texas

cities. They used a methodology copied from the Batelle-Columbus Laboratories in Ohio, which first created such surveys more than twenty years ago.

Although the professors called their approach "grassroots economics" (or sometimes "grassroots industrial policy"), it's still inherently macroeconomic. This is apparent from a report they issued in November 1986, entitled "Rebuilding the Texas Economy." Not surprisingly, Weinstein and Gross called for the creation of yet another blue-ribbon commission to predict various "megatrends" and to chart a course for the future of the Texas economy based on those alleged trends.

Unfortunately, the Weinstein and Gross "Target Industry Surveys" relied heavily on the *Texas Input-Output Model*, issued by the State Water Board. The model was out-of-date when first issued. It was even more inadequate by the time these Cox men used it. So the statistics they relied on to generate their highly mathematical presentation were dubious.

Another disappointment is that their reports are heavily laden with the jargon of econometrics, such as "industry screening matrix," "forward linkages," and "location quotient." Further, the econometric approach is not necessarily related to reality, and especially not to the most important aspects of the real world in Texas.

The problems with their "ivory tower" approach were most obvious in their study of Houston. For example, in 1985 Weinstein and Gross asserted that Houston had an inadequate supply of physicians' offices, osteopaths, chiropractors, optometrists, nursing-care facilities, medical labs, dental labs, and outpatient-care facilities. Houston? One of the best-known cities in the world for the extent and quality of its medical facilities? And at a time when Houston was already deeply into a glut of office space?

The professors correctly condemned such externally oriented economic development efforts as the solicitation of branch plants. But then they advised Houston to become a center for the production of carbonated soft drinks. Yet given the nature of the real world, the only way Houston could do this would be through the very branch plants the professors had condemned.

It is true that Soho Natural Soda, which started in 1977, now has sales of nearly $100 million a year. But Soho is not a Houston company and, by 1985, it had filled one of the very few market niches that the industry giants had ignored. The two economists did not suggest how Houston could realistically proceed on their recommendations in this matter.

"Real World" Survey Paves the Way

The statistics of the Birch studies, already discussed at length, were more empirical than those of Weinstein and Gross. Birch's data corresponded directly to the facts in the business world and in the various economies he analyzed. As to job gains or losses, Birch observed that:

> Most of the variation in the net change is due to the variation in the rate of job generation (births and expansions), not to variation in the rate of loss . . . The findings suggest that it makes little sense to attempt to influence firms to move (in the physical sense), nor is there much opportunity, short of influencing the business cycle, to influence the rate at which firms contract or go out of business. Practically all the leverage lies in affecting where new firms locate and where existing firms choose to expand.

The folks at New Jersey Bell illustrate a mesoeconomic or "bootstrap" approach. As businesses had begun to vanish in New Jersey in the late 1970s, the telephone company was losing customers, both business and residential. Worse, New Jersey Bell had the most extensive facilities in most towns. So when the towns raised their property taxes to cover the revenue shortfalls, New Jersey Bell got hit hard. It was a double whammy.

But instead of waging a bitter political campaign against higher property taxes, the Bell people devised a win-win strategy that has proven enormously successful.

After learning of Birch's 1979 report, they decided to find a way to act on its implications. The result was the nation's first "Business Retention and Expansion Survey." As Steve Heller, New Jersey Bell's administrator for the program, explained, "We feel that if we can make businesses happy where they are and concentrate on small and medium businesses, we will get economic growth."

In 1980 the phone company, working in cooperation with

the New Jersey Business and Industry Association, began its first survey. Two facets were crucial to the program's success:

1. **It was a business-to-business project.** Heller, the survey director, emphasized that the project depended heavily on the private sector, because otherwise local government officials would have too much temptation to politicize the activity.
2. **It was a person-to-person project.** What's more, the particular nature of the people chosen to conduct the survey made all the difference in the world.

The New Jersey Business and Industry association asked for volunteers with business backgrounds to conduct the survey. The survey was not conducted by mail, nor did it rely on students or professional market researchers. Those who came forward often were retired from business. Real estate professionals also got involved in the project, and quite effectively.

In each municipality, target firms were selected on the basis of the SIC (Standard Industrial Classification) Code. Manufacturers received top priority. One hundred to two hundred firms were identified in each locality.

To solicit the cooperation of these businesses, the program directors asked the mayor of each municipality to send out a cover letter to all the firms identified in that municipality. Along with the government leader's letter, they asked for—and got—a cover letter from a very prominent local businessperson, who also encouraged cooperation.

The survey staff then matched the backgrounds of the volunteers with the SIC Code of each identified firm. Often an interviewer had friends managing some of the firms, so he or she would visit those firms. The volunteers first contacted the firms to set up a one-on-one meeting to run through the survey questionnaire. Initially, each interviewer was asked to meet with no more than three establishments, all of which were local.

Volunteers went through a training session before actually visiting the companies. This ensured that they could accurately explain the nature of the survey and would understand how to conduct the interview. The interviewer's respectable standing as a businessperson, often combined with personal acquaintance, enabled the survey to make the most of the meetings. The encounter was very low-key and low-stress, in large part because both the manager and the interviewer were "on the same wavelength."

In all areas of the state, the survey people first asked a common set of questions. Then they proceeded to questions regarding the local situation and the individual firm's particular needs. All information gathered remained confidential with respect to the firm's identity.

The following is a representative sample of the inputs sought:

- Corporate name, and address in the state
- Location of corporate headquarters, if out of state
- List of other corporate locations, and function of facilities at those locations
- Date of firm's founding
- Date firm began operation at this site
- The nature of the firm's business
- Main raw materials used in the firm's manufacturing processes
- Means of transportation used to ship and receive goods
- Impact of foreign and domestic competition
- Impact of energy costs and materials shortages.
- Impact of labor-force quality, labor relations; caliber of the firm's machinery; sufficiency of space for operations; inflation, market condition, or transportation problems
- Ownership of firm's facilities
- If facilities leased, the date lease expires
- Size of facilities
- Location of firm's customers, on a percentage basis: in local municipality, in municipality plus immediate surrounding area, in SMSA (Standard Metropolitan Statistical Area), in surrounding region, in the entire country, and in foreign countries
- Classification of most customers' industry: construction, transportation, printing and publishing, retail trade, consumer goods, petroleum and chemicals, electronics, machinery or tool and die, and miscellaneous
- Location of firm's major competitors, on a rough geographical basis
- Any contact by representatives of another city or state seeking to get the firm to relocate there and, if so, by whom; awareness of the economic development programs in other areas and, if so, which ones
- Plans to move: to where, when, and why; whether had considered

moving at any time in the past, and if didn't move, why not
- Expansion plans at present location
- Equipment modernization plans
- Number of employees, skill levels and wage rates; number of part-time employees; special training required for employees (and how obtained); employee turnover rate; residence of most employees; amount of difficulty in finding qualified employees (and how obtained); how employees commute to work
- Adequacy of water supply and water pressure for firm's facilities
- Adequacy of sanitation
- Recent problems with crime against the firm's employees or property
- Problems with traffic flow in surrounding area or with illegal parking that interferes with firm's operations; problems with street maintenance or flooding of area
- Awareness of, or use of, jobs tax credits, the Small Business Administration, Urban Development Action Grants, State Industrial Revenue Bonds
- Impact of local property taxes, licensing procedures and fees, inspection procedures and fees
- Financing plans: through conventional facilities, federal or state programs, a parent company, venture capital, or internally generated funds
- Name of the firm's bank
- Membership in civic and commercial organizations
- Rating of local municipality as a place to do business; rating of the state
- Suggestions for improvements

This is clearly a very sophisticated and thorough program—and the foregoing questions are but a sampling. That is why the business-to-business and person-to-person nature of the survey was paramount.

New Jersey Bell's "Business Retention and Expansion Survey" adopts, for an economy, what Klein described as essential for success in any given firm: receptivity to negative feedback, openness to hints from the environment, and internalization of risk. The results of the survey are "predictably unpredictable."

Recalling the discussion of Jacobs's model for economic development, the input regarding the location of customers is very important. For Texas, the purchase of an import from New Orleans into Beaumont just might give the Beaumont economy a good candidate for import replacement, for example.

Input from the survey in New Jersey was turned over to the Rutgers University Research Program for Innovation and Productivity Strategies—quite a mouthful, that. Rutgers used a "Statistical Package for Social Sciences" (SPSS) software program to analyze the results in the abstract.

However, for concrete applications, the survey staff called the problems to the attention of municipal officials. Charles Durand, of the New Jersey Department of Commerce, notes that "there is no way a mayor can know all the details of what's happening in his town." The survey especially sought feedback regarding "red flag" problems that needed immediate action by municipal officials. Usually these concerned such things as police protection or water problems.

Because the program relies so heavily on volunteers, the costs of conducting the survey in each municipality are quite modest: the mid-five-digits, at most. The largest survey to date was in the city of Paterson. It took 15 months and covered 440 firms. This was obviously not a "quick fix" program.

It's difficult to point to dramatic examples of the survey's impact. There were some firms that announced they would have left various municipalities had they not been interviewed as part of the survey and resolved their grievances as a result. It must have been a relief to these municipalities to uncover such dissatisfaction and to correct the problems before relocation was underway. (However, as the Birch data show, the loss of firms through relocations is insignificant in terms of the overall employment picture.)

Five years after the project began, the survey had covered forty-two municipalities in New Jersey. Perhaps it's only a coincidence that in 1985 the accounting and management-consulting firm of Alexander Grant & Company moved New Jersey from last place to first in the quality of the manufacturing environment on its list of the six mid-eastern states.

Elizabeth, New Jersey, then followed up with its "Project Team" program. This involves virtually every civic, labor, commercial, and governmental organization in town. Project Team conducts informal and formal get-togethers involving businesspeople, elected officials, department heads of city services, labor leaders, bankers, and others. It keeps track of firms whose leases are due to expire, and offers to assist them in locating elsewhere in town. These are just two of its numerous activities to create a meaningful "pro-business" environment.

Elizabeth also has conducted more business-retention-and-expansion surveys. The subsequent efforts contacted firms that hadn't existed during the first survey, or which hadn't participated. Also, since the first survey only canvassed manufacturers, they then expanded it to include retail establishments and firms in the service industries.

In these areas, phone company officials can honestly say, "Ask not for whom Bell toils—it toils for thee."

Throughout the Frost Belt, there have been other business-retention-and-expansion surveys. However, the purpose seems to have been to prevent corporate relocations and runaway plants. Given Birch's findings, then, they seem to have done the right thing for the wrong reason.

In Texas, we need to concentrate on helping small manufacturing firms to survive—especially to keep those below the watershed mark of twenty employees from disappearing unnecessarily.

Even though the best business-retention-and-expansion survey in the world cannot do anything to reverse a deteriorating market, it can provide both the moral support and a lot of the little things that can give a small-businessperson the incentive to "hang in there." If a small firm is in danger of going out of business, the final straw could be something as trivial as chronic traffic congestion near the firm's loading dock, or a constant runaround from some government department about getting a permit.

Moreover, follow-up programs such as Elizabeth, New Jersey's "Project Team" would enable businesspeople to establish relationships with public officials other than politicians. This alone should make it easier to solve problems that arise, and perhaps even to keep them from arising in the first place. It would certainly reduce the barriers that sometimes exist between businesspeople and civil servants, who tend to move in different worlds and to have different ways of approaching a problem. Last, it would enable businesspeople to avoid having to ask a politician for a favor (which always means giving him or her an I.O.U.).

A small firm that has survived the worst, and is ready to stage a comeback, ought to receive all the support it can use as it begins to expand again. This is especially true because small businesses tend to overreact to economic recovery, and to take on more than they can handle.

Several organizations in various parts of Texas already have conducted what they say are business-retention-and-expansion surveys. However, it appears that virtually all of them have been conducted by mail. This guarantees failure. Most businesspeople do not have the time or inclination to fill out a lengthy questionnaire—and especially not one that asks for a lot of confidential information. The typical response rate to these mail surveys has been around 4 percent.

But even that figure is misleading, because many of the respondents just don't answer the more complicated or revealing questions. In truth, it seems that the organizations that conducted these surveys by mail would have done better to have saved their time and postage. The results they got are nearly useless.

The problem seems to be that the business-retention-and-expansion survey is not a "magic wand" to wave over a local economy to produce an immediate payoff. It does not turn an economy into an "instant winner."

For that reason, it's difficult to get funding to do the survey the right way. The officials in charge often just can't get interested in something that won't make them look very good, very quickly. It's much more fun to spend money on flying to Tokyo to beg the Japanese to build a branch plant here. And of course if the Japanese agree to do so, then there's all the gratifying publicity to prove that the officials are doing their jobs.

The 21st century is just around the corner. We in Texas need to start today to take a long-term approach, and engage in long-term efforts, that will provide for our future prosperity in the long term. Otherwise, we never will be masters of our own fate.

"Bootstrap Economics" Comes Up With a Winner

This is where the "Oregon Marketplace" project is relevant. Oregon in general, and Lane County in particular, are examples of what Jane Jacobs calls a "supply region," explained in chapter 7. This region's economy is even more dependent on the timber industry than Texas is on energy and agribusiness. And the pattern in the timber industry is one of boom and bust.

Between 1978 and 1983, the unemployment rate nearly doubled in Lane County, reaching almost 12 percent. The number of jobs directly related to the timber industry had dropped 27 percent. Since the county had only 250,000 residents and 7,000 businesses, the impact of the downturn was severe.

Eugene is Lane County's seat. Leaders there—like the folks at New Jersey Bell—had learned of Birch's 1979 study, "The Job Generation Process." In 1981 they contracted to have their own local study done. They found that between 1973 and 1980, non-wood-related manufacturing firms with twenty employees had created nearly two-thirds of all the new jobs in Lane County.

The leaders of Eugene felt that if these small businesses could find ways to get even more business, they would add new employees at an even more rapid rate. Since the timber industry was in a recession and laying off employees, Eugene's leaders were eager to act quickly.

Apparently no one in Lane County had read any of Jane Jacobs's books. Yet they gradually developed a program that intuitively used all the basic principles in two of her books, *The Economy of Cities* and *Cities and the Wealth of Nations*. The person who spearheaded the project and carried it through to success was another woman, Alana Probst.

Because most of the local economy was related to the timber industry, Probst realized that Lane County exported wood products and imported non-wood products. She surmised that the local demand for at least some imported products was large enough to justify local production, if the economies of scale were right. Local production instead of imports would 1) keep the money in the local economy that had heretofore left it, and 2) create a lot of new economic activity to offset the decline in the timber industry.

This is exactly what Jacobs's import-replacement multiplier is all about. Since the local economy was depressed, Lane County's leaders knew it would make sense to urge people to "buy local"—but only if locally-made items 1) cost no more than imported ones and 2) were at least as good as the imports.

Probst also saw that it would make sense to find ways to start producing other goods that could replace imports.

The big question was economies of scale: How much production of a given item would be required, in order to match the price of the imports and to match or exceed the imports' quality? This, in turn, revealed the existence of a problem: No one really knew just how much of any item was being imported into Lane County.

This lack of information revealed yet another problem. Many local small firms that produced items that could replace imports simply did not have the resources to aggressively seek out more local buyers. The problem, in part, was—again—a lack of information. Most local producers didn't know who was buying imports that could be replaced by local goods. And the small businesses couldn't afford a full-scale marketing effort to make potential buyers aware of their existence. They didn't have the wherewithal for an advertising campaign or a public relations campaign, nor for sales representatives to locate and call on potential customers.

On the other hand, many small local firms that bought imports did not have the resources to aggressively seek out a potential local manufacturer. Often they did not even have a separate purchasing department. Their business went to the vendors who could afford to make the aforementioned sales efforts—mostly large out-of-state firms. By default, Lane County in particular and Oregon in general were reinforcing their dependence on outsiders by failing to invest in their own economy.

These facts implied two other things, which held the solution to the problems. First, Probst could easily see that goods shipped into Lane County would cost the local buyer more than goods made locally—if all other things were equal. This immediately gave local firms a potential advantage: Even if the local cost of producing was somewhat higher than the cost of the imported good, the shipping cost gave the local producer some extra room for competitiveness.

Second, the sales effort by the out-of-state manufacturers was part of their cost of doing business. They had to recover that cost in pricing their product. So Probst reasoned that, if the local economy could find an inexpensive way to merely cause local producers and local users to become aware of each other's existence, they could dispense with the usual whistles and bells of a full-scale marketing effort.

On a cost/benefit basis, this made enormous sense. By moving this low-key marketing and purchasing program off-site, out of the individual local businesses, it would give local producers another way to keep their prices below those of the firms exporting to Lane County. In fact, because the local businesses that were the target of this program could not afford their own in-house marketing and purchasing departments, the project leaders had no choice but to establish the program on an off-site basis.

When Probst finally got to the heart of the problem, she saw that she had also gotten to the heart of its solution.

It's important to emphasize here and now that the resulting "Oregon Marketplace" project is not a protectionist "buy local" campaign. It is not a program of import substitution but of import replacement, as described in chapter 8.

As with the business-retention-and-expansion surveys by New Jersey Bell, the Oregon Marketplace project starts with field operatives who personally contact local businesses. They ask managers to list products they are importing, whether for use in their own manufacturing process or as items not directly related to production for sale. The interviewers also contact organizations and institutions that are not commercial, but which perhaps also import goods.

Whenever the manager or official interviewed indicates that his or her operation is importing something, the Oregon Marketplace staffer asks if management would be willing to at least look at other sources for those imported items—specifically, at local sources.

Oregon Marketplace simultaneously seeks out local suppliers of goods. Local production might already be used locally, or it might be exported. Either way, the local supplier's existence might not even be known to some potential local customers.

A key consideration is to discover what the local firms *could* produce, as well as what they are producing. The term used to describe this is "hidden diversity." This is another concept that Jane Jacobs had called attention to long ago in her book *The*

Economy of Cities.

In her books, Jacobs describes the way things work, and how and why they happen. What Probst and the Oregon Marketplace sought to do was not to just let things happen, but to make things happen. Their program is much more formal in its operation, more thorough, and hence much more effective than happenstance could achieve.

The Oregon Marketplace program is a voluntary one on the part of participating businesses, just as the business-retention-and-expansion surveys in New Jersey are. No tax incentives or job-credit benefits go to the participants. Yet it works extremely well, and has been quite effective.

When the project gets a "lead" about a potential import replacement, it automatically contacts all of the obvious potential local suppliers. The staff also prepares a circular on a regular basis that goes to all participating businesses that are producers of goods: There just might be some hidden diversity in one of those firms, a potential bidder no one had thought of.

The Payoff at the Bottom Line

There are those who think of economic development as the relocation of a corporate headquarters to their city, or the opening of a branch plant. Such people favor high-budget efforts to lure those corporations (including costly junkets to corporate headquarters or even to foreign countries). They will be disappointed in the success stories that follow. All these illustrations are the results of a simple project in "bootstrap economics."

A Eugene, Oregon, company that manufactures self-inking rubber stamps had been buying $150,000 worth of display cards each year from an out-of-state firm. The buyer, Stampos, had initially sought a supplier in Oregon but hadn't found one. Even when its volume of purchases reached $150,000 it continued with the out-of-state vendor.

But the situation had changed. Stampos now was a successful company and could give someone a much larger volume of business than when Stampos had first sought local vendors. Oregon Marketplace realized this and asked local printers to bid on the job. The local printers had not been interested the first time around because the manufacture of the display cards required special equipment that no local printer owned.

Given the prospect of large orders from a proven company, though, several local printers were now willing to invest the $100,000 required to buy the right equipment. They bid on the job, and Stampos switched its purchases to one of these local firms.

Lane County has a firm in it called Ecklund Construction Company. However, Ecklund Construction's "hidden diversity" included the ability to manufacture metal control boxes for use on irrigation equipment. The Pierce Corporation, in Oregon, makes irrigation equipment. It had been buying metal control boxes from an out-of-state supplier.

When the Oregon Marketplace staff contacted potential suppliers of a replacement for this imported item, they went to sheet-metal and metal-fabrication shops. But the bidding opportunity also was listed in the circular, and Ecklund Construction had the presence of mind to go for it. Ecklund Construction won the contract, valued at $50,000 in its first year and renewed and expanded in subsequent years.

No ribbon-cutting ceremonies here. No television crews showing participants on the evening news. This is strictly a "small potatoes" operation. But those spuds add up. In its first year, as a pilot project, Oregon Marketplace got $1,858,470 in new business for the firms in Lane County. Taking into account the multiplier effect of these initial contracts, officials calculate the total economic impact at $4,464,000.

That may not seem like much to those who like to think on the grand scale that "Texas" has always stood for. And perhaps the actual amount of the multiplier effect (the estimated factor was 2.5) is an exaggeration. But it sure beats a poke in the eye with a sharp stick.

During the pilot project, local businesses also saved $1.5 million that they otherwise would have spent on imports, or on freight charges for imports. Given the fact that a firm is more competitive if it can hold its prices in line, and that it can better hold its prices in line if it can hold its costs down, this is very significant—especially in a recession, when it's a "buyer's market."

The Oregon Marketplace pilot project also was credited with

directly creating 100 new jobs in Lane County. There is no way to measure how many jobs were retained as a result of the project, but it stands to reason that if the project directly caused the creation of 100 new jobs it surely must have indirectly caused the saving of others.

The cost of all this? $35,000. That's thirty-five thousand dollars. The return on the investment, in terms of economic activity, was 5700% in one year. The project was funded by a local bank, by the City of Eugene, and by the Lane County Private Industry Council.

Jacobs Points the Way

Apparently it was only after the pilot project was up and running that the Oregon Marketplace people became aware of the writings of Jane Jacobs. Thanks to Jacobs, they suddenly had an extremely well thought out theoretical justification for what they were doing, backed up by a treasury of examples from other economies.

Most important, Jacobs helped the Oregon Marketplace people to understand the difference between import substitution and import replacement. There had been problems with those who objected to the Oregon Marketplace program as one of protectionist "buy local" discrimination. And, in truth, evidently some of the early participants had seen it that way, too.

Alana Probst and the leaders of Lane County then approached the Oregon legislature. Their project had been a success. With that evidence in hand, plus the thorough analysis provided by Jacobs, Probst and the others could prove that their performance was no fluke. They wanted to extend it throughout Oregon. In 1985 the state legislature, appropriately impressed, funded the expansion. The state put up $450,000, and the private sector came up with matching funds. There now are a dozen regional Oregon Marketplace projects.

In *The Economy of Cities*, published in 1969, Jacobs had maintained that only in cities was there enough existing diversity to make possible "hidden" diversity. However, thanks to computers and telecommunications, twenty years later this is no longer so. Modern technology has made possible a statewide network in Oregon. The regional groups can unite their efforts in a synergistic economic development. This synergy works two ways.

First, if a local importer cannot find a local supplier within the region, the regional staff posts the opportunity on a computer "bulletin board" that all the other regions see. Thus, suppliers in the local area get first crack at the opportunity. If they can't fulfill the need, it's passed on to others. The other regional staffs then include the information in their own circulars the next time they are distributed. This way, even though the ideal solution— keeping local money in the local economy—isn't reached, at least the second-best solution might be: keeping Oregon money in the Oregon economy.

Success Stories Expand Their Reach

The other way in which the synergy works is that many small-scale users of a product can combine their purchases. The computer network makes possible a modern version of the old practice of cooperative buying.

Using the computer network, several jails in Oregon joined forces to buy uniforms for inmates. Each jail bought so few uniforms that no local supplier could make them at a competitive price. When Oregon Marketplace persuaded them to buy cooperatively, the size of their potential order was big enough to cause an Oregon firm to bid on the contract. The Oregon firm's price was better than that of the out-of-state firms that had been supplying the jails separately. It won the order.

Soon, public hospitals in the state began purchasing surgical gowns through a similar cooperative-buying arrangement.

These two examples create two benefits for Oregon taxpayers. One benefit is that they cut costs in the public sector, thus helping these institutions to hold their budgets in line. The other benefit is that they expanded local tax revenues by increasing local economic activity.

The best success story to date involves the unglamorous poultry and food-processing industries. A large food-processing company in Oregon, Chef Francisco, specialized in frozen items. Oregon Marketplace inquired about imports from outside the state, and whether or not management would consider new suppliers from within Oregon. The company replied that it used about 900,000 pounds of chicken base, cubed chicken, chicken fat, and chicken broth each year. A large percentage of its cooked chicken was shipped in from Arkansas.

Ironically, Oregon has a large poultry industry. However, for various reasons, no firm in Oregon had gone the next step and become a poultry processor. As happens so often in Texas, the raw material was being shipped out of state for intermediate processing. In this case, chickens were the raw material. Although the partially processed birds were shipped back in for final processing, much of the value-added was occurring elsewhere, not in Oregon.

The Oregon Marketplace staff contacted poultry operations in Oregon and asked if they'd cook chicken. The firm that was most interested was located only ten miles from the frozen-food company. It took many months for that firm, Willamette Poultry, to study the chicken-cooking business and to evaluate the financial analysis. Finally they decided to go for it.

They won the contract. As a result, Willamette Poultry built a new $1.5 million plant, hired eighty new workers, and increased its sales by nearly a million dollars a year. It sells not only to Chef Francisco's frozen-food operation, but to other smaller processors throughout the state.

The most interesting example involves petrified wood. The Japanese highly prize ceremonial tea sets made from this material. Two firms in Japan that made these sets had heard of Oregon Marketplace, and asked the staff to try to locate a source of petrified wood. The notice went out on the electronic bulletin board, but no firms in Oregon dealt with petrified wood. However, Marketplace staff members asked all their contacts if they knew of any other potential source at all.

The story goes that one staffer mentioned it to a rural gasoline-station owner. The owner said he knew of a rancher who was a recluse but who had a lot of petrified wood on his property. The man didn't have a phone, though. Supposedly the staffer then set out on what he thought would be a wild goose chase, only to discover that the old rancher did indeed have petrified wood—82 tons of it.

This was the first instance where Oregon Marketplace engaged in promotion of exports. The project officially is still concerned only with import replacement. However, it conducts searches for would-be exporters when asked to do so by would-be importers outside Oregon.

Still More Multiplier Effects

What Jacobs calls the import-replacement multiplier is clearly at work in a powerful way as a result of the Oregon Marketplace project. Companies that have been "matched" by the project often expand their business dealings into other product lines. Sometimes a search fails to create a match, initially, because no potential supplier exists in Oregon.

But one of the spin-off effects of the Oregon Marketplace program has been a surge in entrepreneurship. This is because one of the biggest problems that entrepreneurs have is identifying their market and knowing how to effectively reach that market. With the Oregon Marketplace, potential entrepreneurs have the market handed to them: a bird's nest on the ground.

Not surprisingly, what happens fairly often is that new firms arise to take advantage of proffered opportunities. And, as already mentioned, existing firms sometimes engage in corporate "intra-preneurship" to expand into a new product line or service in response to an Oregon Marketplace inquiry.

Further in keeping with Jacobs's conclusions, firms that start out by supplying to the local market, or contributing items to a product manufactured and sold by another firm, often end up becoming exporters. Echo Spring Water has begun to establish itself nationwide. Echo Spring Water is an offshoot of Echo Spring Dairy, which modified its milk-bottling operations to supply bottled water to the local market as a result of an Oregon Marketplace inquiry.

It bears repeating that the Oregon Marketplace is not a protectionist program. Nor is it a "business roundtable" organization, where firms become members and restrict membership to just one firm in each industry and then pledge to buy only from fellow members. As two officials involved in the project explained:

> A participating company has sole right to choose any or none of the bids submitted. No obligation exists to switch to a local

supplier unless it makes good business sense. ... The program does not operate for the benefit of any particular supplier or would-be supplier. It does not require that local bidders be given a preference—just that they be given a chance. Once buyers have the bids in hand, the decision of whether to use a new supplier is theirs alone.

The Oregon Marketplace project also has produced benefits that weren't anticipated. For example, "just in time" inventory control methods are gaining popularity in America. This system works best when the supplier is close at hand, because demand for input can vary and time in transit is worthless to both parties. Replacing imports with local production means that manufacturers can more easily take advantage of this system.

Quality control also has received more attention in America than in years past. The presence of local vendors means that the buyer can easily check work in process and oversee changes in equipment resulting from new specifications.

This book has been critical of branch plants as an alleged solution to a local economy's problems. However, an import-replacement program in connection with a branch plant can improve what might otherwise be a counterproductive situation.

All corporations want to be "good citizens" in the local community. But branch plants are part of a large organization that has well-established logistics. So the branch plants have little incentive to establish their own programs of seeking out local items for input other than the obvious ones such as telephone and electrical service.

With a successful import-replacement program such as the Oregon Marketplace, the branch plant can easily contribute more to the local economy, indirectly and to its own immediate benefit, than it does at present. The manager might even gain recognition within his or her firm by discovering a local source that is better than the present one for the entire corporate network.

As chapter 8 showed, branch plants can cause the local economy to become dependent on outsiders, if the local economy is small relative to the branch plant's impact. And if the local economy is dependent on that facility, people might easily gravitate toward the plant instead of setting up businesses of their own.

At first it might seem that an import-replacement program in conjunction with a branch-plant operation will make the local economy even more dependent on that branch plant. However, the new import-replacement businesses give the local economy the potential to get out of its rut, because of the import-replacement multiplier and the export multiplier. At least a deliberate import-replacement program gives the local economy a chance at diversifying and becoming independent. Otherwise, it is hopelessly vulnerable.

Even those who refuse to be weaned from their devotion to corporate relocation efforts have something to gain from an import-replacement program. If the corporation is a manufacturer, it will most likely have suppliers in its current location. These suppliers usually stay behind, of course. Perhaps the manufacturer will then import their products into its new location.

Yet it would seem likely that the manufacturer would prefer to have local suppliers in its new location, at least for some items. Granted, "economic development" people would, in such a case, try to find local suppliers for the items in question. But with an on-going import replacement program already up and running, their work would be made so much easier. They could then concentrate on what they want to do most: wooing potential transplants to their area—for what little that effort is worth.

The Oregon Marketplace data bank for bidding opportunities is constantly updated, and unfilled requests are retained. If no supplier is available at the time of the initial request, perhaps at some later date a willing entrepreneur will come forward or a corporation will decide to try its hand at "intra-preneurship" to meet the need. Just because resources weren't available earlier doesn't mean they won't be available later. As long as the willing customer is still in business, that opportunity stays on-line.

The Oregon Marketplace has had some failures, of course. Sometimes, even with the reduction in freight charges, the local firms just can't offer a competitive price. Perhaps the would-be supplier does not yet have enough financial stability for the would-be customer. Or maybe the buyer runs into financial difficulties and has to cancel the bidding request. Sometimes a firm that had been buying from outsiders decides to make the item in-house instead, thus changing its mind after filing a request for a local-supplier search.

There was even one case where a company got so much business as a result of being matched with customers that it complained bitterly to the Oregon Marketplace staff about the added workload! A lot of firms in Texas would welcome that problem.

But the project already has been so successful that it's spun off another project: the New Business Generator. This program tries to identify, and then work with, potential entrepreneurs in groups normally ignored for this function: the disabled, older people, minorities, and the unemployed. The economy benefits, society benefits, and of course the new entrepreneurs themselves benefit—both materially and psychologically. Granted, this too is only "small potatoes." But adding them all up gives us a lot of food for thought.

In Texas, for example, there is a very large population of ex-convicts who have difficulty finding jobs. Even when they do get work, they often carry the stigma of "ex-con" with them. But a small start-up firm, composed entirely of former prisoners, might give these men and women a chance to go straight for good. On the one hand, they'd never have to worry about being discriminated against because of their past (at least, not by others in the company). On the other hand, they might prove much more successful as entrepreneurs than they ever would as employees. At the very least, they would gain self-respect, and thus would perhaps lose the resentment against society that seems to prompt disrespect for the law.

The Oregon Marketplace is not the closely guarded bureaucratic turf of some self-serving political appointees. It works only because it is an open network. It involves chambers of commerce, business and trade and professional groups, elected officials, civic groups, banks and other lending institutions, utilities, and the media.

As is clear from the previous example, the New Jersey business-retention-and-expansion surveys would dovetail perfectly with Marketplace-type projects.

A Rose to San Antone

So far, the City of San Antonio is the only Texas municipality that seems to be both aware of and interested in the Oregon Marketplace. A delegation from the city visited Oregon to view the project first hand in 1988. As of this writing, they are trying to get budget approval to set up such a program in San Antonio. Gayl S. Maring, a business development specialist in the marketing division of the city's Department of Economic and Employment Development, is coordinating the Marketplace plans.

However, the city already has a "Buy San Antonio" campaign underway. Unfortunately, the campaign at first appeared to be—and perhaps was intended as—a protectionist effort. The "Oregon Marketplace" project made the same mistake, initially. Yet the people in Oregon overcame that mistake—as will the folks in San Antonio.

Blueprint for Texas Agricultural Recovery

Actually, one effort already is well underway in Texas that resembles the Oregon Marketplace. Ironically, it's a project in the sector of our economy which typically has the lowest value-added of all: agriculture. This, however, also makes that sector the most logical place to look for opportunities to boost value-added.

In October 1986, the Texas Department of Agriculture issued a report entitled *Economic Growth through Agricultural Development: A Blueprint for Action.* The blueprint applied to both food and non-food aspects of agriculture. In terms of bootstrap economics, the report sought import replacement, product innovation, and higher value-added.

A greater irony about this project is that it's the creation of Jim Hightower, the state commissioner of agriculture, who has a well-deserved reputation as a liberal—when "liberal" is thought to be a synonym for "anti-business." Yet despite measures by various public officials to promote the image of Texas as a "pro-business" state, Hightower has been the only major elected official to try to make it a reality. The "blueprint" program helps Texas businesspeople to help themselves—in a way that benefits all of us instead of further enriching a few at the expense of the many (especially the taxpayers).

With regard to foods, Hightower's import-replacement program focuses largely on pinto beans, Oriental vegetables, and sprouts. For example, until the start of the program, most pinto beans sold in Texas were imported from Colorado. This represents a potential of $17 million in added revenues for Texas farmers, and that's based solely on the present market. If the current popularity of "Tex Mex" food takes hold outside of Texas, the gain will be much larger.

A second area of agricultural development of foodstuffs involves the promotion of new products, such as blueberries and wine. Crawfish and catfish farming are other new endeavors.

One of the most appealing features about the Texas Department of Agriculture program is that it urges farmers to diversify without abandoning the crops they're presently growing. Instead of switching completely from, say, wheat to pinto beans, farmers are encouraged to grow both wheat and pinto beans. That way, the farmer can escape from being completely dependent on the market price for just one commodity. Such diversification also provides each farmer with a hedge against potential disaster in any one crop.

Added economic insurance comes from non-food products, such as Christmas trees. Even the traditional nuisance, mesquite, is becoming a cash crop. Its popularity for backyard grilling and as a non-oil preparation of gourmet cuisine continues to grow.

The Agriculture Department's efforts include promoting value-added endeavors, especially the processing and packaging of crops and animal products. Overall, Texas is the nation's second-largest agricultural state. Yet food and animal processing here is only 6 percent of the national total. This is especially dismaying because Texas is a major center for the production of plastic packaging materials.

The Department of Agriculture has already helped to start processing projects such as a flour mill, an aseptic fruit-juice facility, and a hide-tanning plant. In its first year, the "blueprint" programs had 108 projects in the works. These were intended to provide 8300 jobs and to keep (or bring) $720 million in(to) Texas. The total impact of a vertically integrated pinto bean value-added program, for example, is $66 million a year.

As Hightower explained:

Rather than spending all of our time, energy and money trying to lure General Motors or Toyota to come build a factory for us, it should be state policy to invest in the genius of our own people—in their neighborhoods, in their towns and cities, and on their farms and ranches. Rather than trickle-down economics, this is percolate-up economics, generating true growth and prosperity at the grassroots level.

What Hightower calls "percolate-up" economics is here called "bootstrap" economics—or, more formally, "meso-economics." He continues:

All of these are down-to-earth, grunt-level, here-and-now profitable enterprises that Texans themselves can plant and grow throughout the state. Added together, these small and medium-sized agricultural ventures will help create the new income and the new jobs that the Texas economy must have tomorrow if we are to grow out of today's economic stagnation.

Hightower isn't the only one, of course, who's involved in such efforts. Texas A&M has been hard at work on such matters, too.

The Texas 1015 Supersweet onion was developed at A&M's Texas Agricultural Experimental Station, and has been welcomed with open arms (and dry eyes) in kitchens everywhere. The economic impact of this new crop is estimated at $200 million in the Rio Grande Valley, alone.

A&M also has supported the development of a new apple industry in Texas—an industry so new that its potential is as yet unknown. However, there's already a Southwest Texas Apple Growers Association, and it has a very savvy marketing strategy.

Another major project is the result of twenty-eight years of research by Dr. Richard Hensz, director of the Citrus Center at another school, Texas A&I University. This is the famous Rio Red (or ruby red) grapefruit. It's touted not only as "the grapefruit of the future," but as the "savior of the Texas citrus industry," which had been destroyed by a killer freeze in 1983.

Fish farming is another activity that's increasing in Texas, apparently with little university or government involvement. And the most interesting new activity of all is *ostrich* farming. Seems that ostrich feathers, ostrich hides, and ostrich meat are all quite valuable. Until quite recently, South Africa had a monopoly in the industry. Now some Texans are looking to break that monopoly. If they succeed, they will not only make their own fortunes but improve the fortunes of Texas.

Maybe this is the place to suggest three other potential agriculture opportunities, apparently as yet unexplored.

The first is that yuppie favorite, sushi. This requires rice, *nori* (a type of seaweed), and fresh fish or cooked shrimp. Texas easily can supply all three in abundance. In a restaurant, sushi costs three dollars or more for just one roll. The market for packaged sushi to be sold in grocery stores must be quite large.

The second is snails. Apparently France has reached the limit of its capacity to supply snails to the world's gourmets. The market for escargot in Asia has been booming in recent years, and the French can't supply it all themselves. Firms in the Orient have been providing home-grown snails to the restaurants there. However, the native species is not nearly as good as the French—according to those who know, which excludes this writer.

The French species will not grow in the Orient. But it will grow in California, where entrepreneurs have turned to snail farming. Just as California vintners have found soil and climate conditions just right for competing with French wines, so have California snail farmers found them right for competing with French snails.

And, of course, Texas vintners have also found that they can compete—both with the French and with the Californians. It seems highly likely that the soil and climate conditions here could support an escargot industry. However, the snails would have to be kept under close watch so they wouldn't make a run for it and escape to people's gardens, as they did in California. So far, the Californians have not expanded their supply enough to meet the need of the market. And this is a high value-added product because it is a gourmet item.

A third possibility is in mariculture, ocean farming. Again, California is the leader. A marine biologist there discovered that offshore oil rigs provide a perfect "bed" for mussels and other shellfish. Oddly, the quantity and quality of the harvest is superior to that of natural locations.

Oil companies were spending a small fortune to clean barnacles from offshore oil rigs. The California mariculture companies first replace inedible shellfish with edible ones, and then harvest them regularly. It's a win-win situation, one that might work in the Gulf.

Texas agriculture has a very important role to play in the future of our economy. But we need to extend efforts such as Hightower's to other sectors of the economy. The programs in New Jersey and Oregon show how to do this.

As previous chapters have emphasized, it is counterproductive to try to eliminate imports altogether. However, it is enormously beneficial to engage in import replacement wherever possible. There are products that will always be made best by those outside Texas. But there are many products now being made outside Texas that we Texans could produce ourselves, at the same or better quality and at the same or better price. Many of these products use inputs from Texas as their raw materials. And at least some items now imported by Texans could be made here and exported instead.

We will never reach a point where we don't need other economies, of course. Nor should we. But that doesn't mean we shouldn't try to be economically self-reliant, in the sense of no longer being subservient to and dependent on others, as their economic colony. We need to build economic independence, in the same way in which we speak of an individual becoming independently wealthy.

And who knows? Perhaps in many industries Texas firms can become recognized as leaders, producers of the highest quality at the best prices. Proper implementation of a Texas Marketplace project, along with a series of properly done business-retention-and-expansion surveys over the years, would be a big step in that direction.

The initials "M.I.T." are known throughout the world. But someday, they just might stand for "Made In Texas": the ultimate in competitive economic performance.

12 Texas as a Welfare State

> ... [T]he real issue facing the United States is not how little or how much the government does, but what the government does, and how it affects economic performance.
>
> —Burton Klein
> *Dynamic Economics*

The chapter on "Growth vs. Development" presented Jane Jacobs's discussion of what she called a "supply region." A supply region depends on exports for its livelihood. In the passage that heads the chapter on "Money vs. Wealth," T.R. Fehrenbach indicates that another term for "supply region" is "economic colony."

Texas has always been an economic colony for the rest of the United States, and the world. Most of the formal economic "development" efforts underway now in this state are unwittingly designed to make Texas even more of an economic colony. Boosting exports, instead of replacing imports, is one of the clearest examples of this wrong-headed approach.

Another one is the solicitation of branch plants. To recapitulate the earlier comments: Branch plants are not necessarily a bad thing; the key concern is the degree to which the activity in question will impinge on the local economy.

If a branch plant dominates the local economy, then it will prove counterproductive in the long run. Just as one shareholder can effectively dominate a corporation while holding far less than a majority of the stock, so can one economic activity dominate an economy without being the only game in town. The multiplier is especially important. A local economy can become utterly dependent on the branch plant—not despite the money a branch plant pumps into the economy, but because of it.

The clearest economic analogy to a branch plant is a plantation. A branch plant may use factory hands instead of field hands, but it's still based on manual labor. And it makes the local economy the "ward" of a distant corporate headquarters.

Economic dependence is similar to dependence on drugs or alcohol or tobacco: It is addictive. In the case of individual human beings, we can see the debilitating effects quite clearly, no matter how exhilarating the "high" induced in the short run. And just as people who are addicted to cocaine, for example, will argue that they can "control" their habit, so the people of an economy addicted to cash infusions from the outside world will argue that they are really masters of their own fate.

But they are not masters of their fate, regardless of whether their livelihood comes from manufacturing in a branch plant or from exports of crops or raw materials. This truth quickly becomes obvious when the corporate headquarters closes the branch plant, or when the world prices of the commodities fall. And, sadly, just as a drug addict who's suddenly lost his source will scramble for the next "fix" rather than go "cold turkey," so do local economic leaders scramble to find a new source for the next economic "fix" rather than undergo economic "treatment."

Although Texas has used oil and agribusiness as its largest source of cash infusion in the 20th century, throughout this state's history the largest source of all has been the federal government. In fact, these two major industries themselves have been heavily dependent on federal subsidies, such as the oil-depletion allowance and agricultural price supports.

Now that both the energy and agribusiness industries are in bad shape, we Texans have scrambled harder and faster than ever to get the federal government to help us out. Today the emphasis has shifted to space and the military.

War and the Welfare State

The South in general, and Texas in particular, have always had a "macho" complex with respect to the armed forces. This is yet another similarity we share with most Third World countries. The tinhorn dictators of most of those other places know quite well that without a strong military they would be out of power quite rapidly. Americans, in contrast, value military spending as a form of economic stimulus.

This attitude is based on a misreading of our experience during the presidency of Franklin Roosevelt. It is well known that the New Deal did not bring America out of the "Great" Depression. That occurred only with the start of war materiel production for World War II. But, as so often happens when people look only at short-run statistical trends rather than at the realities behind the statistics, economists and non-economists alike continue to make hasty generalizations based on faulty extrapolations of the 1941-45 data.

The hardware of World War II consisted mostly of civilian-type goods diverted for use in combat, and especially for combat-support roles. The trucks, planes, and Liberty ships that carried soldiers and supplies to the war zones were very similar to their counterparts in the civilian sector. Even though they initially were constructed for war, their uses carried over to peacetime. The same is true for most of the facilities in which this materiel was produced.

The "Big Inch" and "Little Inch" pipelines were built during World War II to carry the Southwest's oil to the Northeast's refineries that had been built before the war. Those refineries turned the crude oil into gasoline, and into aviation and naval fuels. But civilian vehicles could use those fuels just as easily as military transport, with no modification. And so, after the war, the technological infrastructure, including the pipelines, was in place. This fixed capital provided an important part of the foundation for the huge postwar expansion of the U.S. automobile, aviation, and shipping industries.

The same is true of almost every war industry of those years. There were stunning advances in communications, medicines, cybernetics, plastics, and other petrochemicals such as artificial rubber. But all were advances that the civilian economy would have needed sooner or later, and would have developed sooner or later. The only exception to this was, of course, the armaments themselves.

Yet many of these, such as large bombers, yielded technological innovations and required fixed investment that were invaluable for the civilian economy after the war. What made military production for World War II so beneficial was not that it provided jobs and money, but that it provided the happy accident of capital resources that were then in place for the economy's postwar development.

Times have changed. The technology of war today is so highly complex and specialized that it has virtually no civilian applications. If the nature of military production for World War II had been like the nature of military production today, the economic benefit of all that war spending would have been minimal and short-lived. The opportunity cost of that enormous use of funds indeed would have caused the postwar recession some feared at the time.

Most of America's leaders today experienced their formative years around the time of World War II and the early postwar period. Back then, America had it all. The economies of all the other nations on earth lay in shambles, or else had never developed much in the first place. Our exports expanded into a vacuum waiting to be filled. Our production technology won the war, then provided the basis for an amazing economic expansion.

It's easy to appreciate that our leaders are reluctant—or perhaps completely unable—to part with the outlook they acquired in those halcyon days. Unfortunately, those days were but a brief and glorious interlude, a discontinuity from the usual historical pattern. Even more unfortunately, our leaders have passed the conventional wisdom on to their protegees, who will be our leaders of tomorrow.

The discussion in this chapter to a large extent parallels the theme of Paul Kennedy's book, *The Rise and Fall of the Great Powers*. However, his work has some serious flaws. The result is that the implicit recommendations of his book are quite different from the explicit recommendations which follow here.

By definition, the gross national product (GNP) is the sum of all expenditures for consumption, government programs, investment, and net exports. (But because America's trade "balance" has been negative for many years now, this last item reduces our GNP, year after year.) We tend to treat any increase of GNP as a good thing in itself, just as we tend to treat a surplus in the balance of payments as a good thing in itself. This bias persists even when the increase in GNP is mostly the result of government deficit spending.

Today, one of the largest items of government expenditures at the federal level is for the military.

Conservatives had a field day in the late 1960s and early '70s, charging that liberals were trying to solve each social problem by throwing money at it. The conservatives were correct in that eventually we realized that this liberal approach was failing. But today conservatives are trying to solve our defense problem by throwing money at it.

Certainly no one will argue the point that it is always better to be safe than sorry in matters of potential war. It's also best to be clearly ready, willing, and able to fight and win a war—and thus to discourage aggression. So, better too much than too little with respect to defense spending. And, it is impossible to determine how much military spending really is enough. After all, as long as a well-armed avowed enemy exists, national security will remain a matter of probabilities, not certainty.

However, just as there is a difference between money and real wealth, so there is a difference between national defense and national security. Conservatives are doing the same thing with respect to the armed forces that liberals in the JFK-LBJ years did with respect to social policies: They fail to think through the relationship between ends and means. Further, in the case of the conservatives, they have not even set forth exactly what the ends are, what they are trying to accomplish. Instead, they speak only in terms of "defense," without defining what constitutes an adequate defense.

Last, and worst, neither the liberals nor the conservatives are as concerned about their alleged respective agendas as they are about using budgets for those agendas as a way of buying votes.

Although we will here look at federal spending for the military, this is only because in recent years it's the conservatives who've dominated the national agenda. In the Kennedy-Johnson years it was the liberals, and their spending practices were at least as harmful from an economic perspective.

It really doesn't make much difference whether a massive federal budget is used for conservative programs or for liberal programs. The plain fact is that real wealth, which provides the money to pay for either of these programs, does not grow on trees. But as long as people continue to accept money at face value, Washington will keep handing it out. In the securities market and in real estate this is known as "the theory of the 'greater fool.'"

Our federal budget deficits in recent years have grown staggeringly large. Many observers see no harm in this, and point to the story of Chicken Little (of all things) and his alarmist cry, "The sky is falling!"

A better allusion would be to the story, "The Boy Who Cried 'Wolf!'" Both the liberals and the conservatives have cried "Wolf!" with respect to the other side, when they themselves have been out of power. But, in the fairy tale, there was no wolf until the very end of the story. In our economy, the wolf has always been present—slowly devouring our economic future. However, our wolf is within the body politic, not somewhere outside.

Others comment that inflation has subsided, so all the scare talk about federal deficits is thereby refuted. It's as though a dam were slowly cracking open, about to burst, while these people scoff at warnings of disaster and say, "It hasn't burst yet. Therefore it never will burst."

Skeptics would do well to consult a 1987 book by Alfred Malabre Jr. He's the economics editor of the *Wall Street Journal.* Malabre's work is entitled *Beyond Our Means.* The subtitle is instructive: *How America's Long Years of Debt, Deficits, and Reckless Borrowing Now Threaten to Overwhelm Us.*

The argument that inflation has subsided, and therefore we do not need to worry, is based on some very short-term statistics. But we must look at the realities behind those statistics.

The first is that what the skeptics miss—or, perhaps, choose to ignore—is that our trade deficits have grown staggeringly large in recent years. It's the trade deficits that have restrained inflation.

Inflation results from "too much money chasing too few goods." Economists who belong to the "monetarist" school say that the Federal Reserve controls the money supply, and thus can keep the economy from overheating. But the monetarists have conveniently forgotten the fact that in 1982 the Federal Reserve Board of Governors announced that henceforth they would not even try to control the money supply. Electronic funds transfers and the globalization of financial markets have long since made it impossible for any American central banker to do anything but talk about inflation.

Fortunately, the prestige and influence of the Federal Reserve is still sufficient that even mere words can still have some effect. But if and when push comes to shove, the Federal Reserve will be just as helpless as the rest of us.

There's too much money, in the form of federal deficits, circulating in the American economy. There also are too few goods being produced in the American economy. Inflation has subsided because a huge proportion of the money Washington pumps into the American economy gets sucked right out again—in the form of payment for imports.

A trade deficit of $150 billion in any given year represents the removal from the American economy of $150 billion in that year. If the federal budget deficit is $200 billion, payments for imports cut the inflationary impact by three-fourths. Foreign exports to the United States aren't part of our GNP; they're part of the exporters' GNP. Our money isn't chasing our goods; it's chasing theirs. That money goes into their economies, not ours.

The second thing the skeptics ignore is even more ominous than the first: Our federal deficit is now funded mostly by foreigners. The Japanese alone finance more than a third of the budget deficit. Countries that have large export surpluses with us can, if they choose, recycle some of that surplus in the form of loans to the United States.

In effect, these nations are lending America the money with which we are buying their exports, because the federal-deficit money eventually goes into the hands of consumers—who spend a lot of that money on imports.

This brings us back to the idea of economic independence. The practices outlined above make us doubly dependent on foreign countries: first, by relying on their production of material goods to provide for our standard of living; and second, by relying on their financial institutions to rescue us from being taxed to death by our own government in order to finance ever-increasing federal budgets.

Insofar as much of our federal budget goes to supposedly increase our national defense, this pattern hardly seems to contribute to any increase in our national security at all.

The Past as Future?

Those who are familiar with the history of the Old South will immediately recognize the similarity to the "furnishing merchants" of days gone by. Farmers harvested their crops once a year. But they never had enough money left over after selling their crops to see them through until the next harvest.

The farmers bought all their inputs for agricultural production, and all their consumer goods, from the furnishing merchants in town. The furnishing merchants not only charged high prices, they also charged high rates of interest on credit sales. In part, this was because they in turn were paying a lot of interest on money borrowed from local banks to lend to the farmers. And the local southern banks were paying high interest to borrow this money from the big northern banks.

But the farmers had to do much of their buying on credit. An increasing percentage of their proceeds from selling each year's harvest had to go to the furnishing merchants just to pay the interest on the previous year's purchases. Often there was interest on the interest, and the total from one year would be carried over as an opening balance to the next year's debts. This vicious circle is why so many people east of the Sabine scrawled "G.T.T." ("Gone To Texas") on their shacks and skipped out for the Lone Star State. The merchants then foreclosed on the abandoned farms and became big landowners.

In the same manner, Japan is becoming a large owner of American assets. Some of our biggest industrial corporations and financial institutions no longer can provide for their own capital needs through American sources. But the Japanese can meet those capital needs easily—in return for partial or complete ownership of the American firms. By buying control of the U.S. firms, the Japanese leverage their wealth and gain even more influence over our economy. This gives them a lot of clout with the U.S. government.

It's said that "he who pays the piper calls the tune." The Japanese are approaching the point where they not only pay the piper, they own the pipes he's playing—and can repossess the instrument at any time.

At least the farmers in the Old South had somewhere to go to try to escape their increasing misery. And at least they had a decent excuse: After all, they didn't have the capital or know-how to try to find a better way of making a living. Ironically, today the situation is just the reverse: We have no excuse; we also have nowhere to go. Yet we are deliberately promoting the same vicious circle, in our trade with Japan.

The ramifications of this vicious circle are far worse than what happened to the farmers in the Old South, though, partly because the implications aren't so noticeable today.

It's as true for international relations in particular as it is for life in general, that you don't get something for nothing. In return for the continued financing of our government's deficits by foreigners, our leaders have apparently agreed to accept the strings that are attached.

For example, we do not know just how much of the American economy is now controlled by foreigners. When Congress recently considered a bill to require disclosure of foreign ownership of American tangible business assets, the bill was defeated. Heavy lobbying by the agents of foreign owners largely accounted for the defeat. In a recent article in the business magazine *Manhattan, inc.*, Edward Klein (not to be confused with Burton Klein) quoted one American representative of Japanese interests as follows:

> Bridgestone has bought Firestone and Yasuda Life has bought a chunk of Paine Webber and Dainippon Ink and Chemicals has bought Reichhold Chemicals and Bank of Tokyo has bought the Union Bank of California—you know, the kind of transactions you read about in the newspapers. But that's only the tip of the iceberg.

And the Japanese do not want us to know just how big the iceberg is below the surface. The informant continues:

> Now ... they're positioning themselves for the big push into the future. They're going at it in their own methodical way ... Their targets are financial service companies, chemical companies, auto-parts companies, food processors and distributors. These target companies are all over the country.

Granted, Edward Klein's source was anonymous. So perhaps we should take the statements with a grain of salt. But the writer

Texas as a Welfare State • 161

then quotes Yoshio Terasawa, whom he identifies as "the ranking member of the World Bank Group":

> We have no transcendent precepts or principles that bar us from taking whatever action is necessary. We can be terribly immoral if necessary. Now, in order to make more money and be more competitive, Japanese businessmen will do anything they have to. There are no limits. They may talk about Americanizing their companies to please their American employees, but that is not what they will really do.

That amazingly frank statement is certainly food for thought, especially for those economic-development experts who continue to welcome Japanese businessmen with open arms. Perhaps, though, Terasawa is some sort of aberration, and not truly representative of "Japan, Inc." However, at the end of his article, Edward Klein quotes Walt W. Rostow, who's very much a member of the American establishment and hardly a crank:

> The Japanese have been conducting economic warfare against us, and some very powerful Japanese have loved the game. They're laughing all the way to the bank.

Smiling is more like it, and not just to the bank but to a position of world power as #1. When Japan "reluctantly agreed" to begin production of the FSX fighter plane in Japan, many Americans were concerned that this could be the start of an eventual Gaullist program in Japan. (Charles DeGaulle took France out of NATO, developed a nuclear war capability for France, and generally thumbed his nose at the United States and American interests.)

But the people who voiced such concerns were condemned as "Japan-bashers." It's interesting that no such biased term exists to describe those who are apologists for Japan—perhaps the "Japan Lobby"?

Japan already has about 50 destroyer-type warships, and soon will have 10 more. In contrast, our own Seventh Fleet (in the Pacific) has a total of about two dozen such ships. Japan already has about 300 modern interceptor aircraft—the same number America has to defend the entire continental United States. Japan soon will have the third-largest military in the world. Those who say the Japanese ought to remilitarize just aren't aware of how much Japan has remilitarized.

In commercial matters, Japan always starts at the low end and gradually works up the value-added scale. First motorcycles, eventually high performance automobiles. First transistor radios, eventually high-definition televisions. First semiconductor chips, eventually supercomputers. It seems quite possible that the same thing is happening with regard to Japan's military. The Japanese are gradually becoming self-reliant militarily as well as economically.

There are those who say, "It's about time." And they have a valid point. But they ignore another point that's more important. Since World War II our bargaining leverage with Japan has depended on two facts: First, America was Japan's guardian against aggression; second, America was Japan's prime market for exports. Soon Japan will not need a guardian. And Japan is now America's prime source of capital.

In short, it is quite possible that we already need the Japanese more than they need us. It's said that "nations have no permanent allies, only permanent interests." Can we be so sure that it will remain in Japan's interest to be our ally?

Today, many of the most respected economists in America, liberal and conservative, are saying—with a straight face—that we Americans can, in effect, have our cake and eat it too. But that is possible only because of the Japanese.

While we support enormous budgets to supposedly guard the front door against the Russians, we refuse to acknowledge that the Japanese are carrying everything out the back. And they're financing the mortgage on the house.

In return for Japan's continued financing of our federal deficit, Washington apparently has implicitly agreed to the continuing "de-industrialization" of America, because this vicious circle is a dynamic, ever-expanding process, not a temporary stopgap transaction. Domestically, this means that America must continue to shift from high-wage manufacturing jobs to low-wage service jobs—hence the proliferation of fast-food franchises, the entertainment industry, and group therapy.

Granted, doctors, lawyers, and at least some MBAs will

continue to do well financially. But the doctors will be getting paid by the federal government, the others by the Japanese. Yet this is what the experts and keepers of the conventional wisdom have endorsed as the service economy of the "post-industrial society."

Then again, there are those who say that there's nothing to worry about because the Japanese are building so many factories, from scratch, in America. In other words, the Japanese are re-industrializing America! Key sectors of our economy, and key firms in several of our most important states (especially New York and California) will thus be in the hands of those who do not necessarily have America's best long-run interest at heart.

As economic historian Harold G. Vatter pointed out in his book *The U.S. Economy in World War II*, a lot of American corporate executives were reluctant to cooperate with the war effort or refused to do so altogether. Even if this country faces no threat of another war like World War II, the fact remains that there are times when Washington needs the cooperation of corporate America.

We have no guarantee that Japanese corporations in America will prove cooperative. And if those corporations dominate key industries in our economy, we have a big problem.

Industrial Strength and Military Power

America has been burning its economic candle at both ends for some time now, trying to compete militarily with the Soviet Union and commercially with Japan. In trying to play both ends against the middle, we're losing both contests.

With respect to the Russians, this isn't simply a matter of troop strength, naval forces, air power, nuclear warheads, and the usual litany so dear to the hearts of conservatives. Rather, it's a matter of industrial strength.

In the same way that we Americans look only at the dollar figures involved in the balance of trade, we look only at the dollar figures involved in the gross national product. As far as the conventional wisdom is concerned, $10 million spent on a million copies of Michael Jackson's latest album is worth just as much as $10 million spent on one new factory. $100 million spent on "Cabbage Patch" dolls counts just as much as $100 million spent on technological R&D. The Japanese don't look at things that way, and neither do the Russians.

Edward Jay Epstein, in his recent book *Deception*, indicates that, for the Soviet Union, what counts is industrial strength. Forty years ago, the Russians produced one-tenth as much oil as the United States; they now produce 50 percent more. Forty years ago, their annual production of natural gas was 2 percent of ours; now it's twice as much. Forty years ago, their production of steel each year was one-fourth ours; today it's more than double what we produce. The Soviet merchant marine is the biggest and perhaps the best in the world. America's sank a long time ago.

The backbone of war preparedness is industrial strength. The Russians have it. The Japanese have it. Whether we have it now is debatable.

Those who say that nuclear weapons make war obsolete have ignored the possibility that nuclear weapons make conventional war all the more necessary. Prudent leaders do not take the words of a foreign leader at face value. Rather, they look to that country's capabilities. As individuals, we cannot read one another's minds, even the minds of fellow Americans. How then can we discern the intentions of the leaders of another country? As long as a foreign country has the capability to inflict conventional military devastation upon others, then such action must be considered a realistic possibility.

It does no good to argue that forty years ago the Russian economy was a shambles and therefore its gains are overly dramatized. Nor would the same argument work with respect to Japan. And, while we clearly hold a lead in some high technology fields, we do not hold nearly as much of a lead as is commonly believed. In some areas, even the Russians are equal to or ahead of us.

So what if the average Russian has to wait in a long line for bread and meat? The Russian government is a dictatorship and the Soviet Union is a police state. The recent elections of representatives means little, because the body to which the representatives were elected is powerless. The men in the Kremlin don't have to worry about the fact that consumer goods are in short supply.

While we have very nearly allowed some of our most important basic industries to die (machine tools being the best example), the Russians—like the Japanese—have a well thought out schedule of priorities. And, despite all the talk of *glasnost* and *perestroika*, the Russian economy is still built on warmaking potential.

How long can America remain a military superpower, if we become an economic has-been? Perhaps the British can tell us.

The real trade-off in our economy isn't between "guns" and "butter." It's between money and real wealth. That means we must restore the productivity of our defense industries as well as of our basic industries and our consumer-goods industries. (Nippon Steel, all by itself, spends more each year on research and development than the entire U.S. steel industry does.)

Today in America, however, there is a fundamental difference between military production and civilian production. The difference goes back to the years of the presidency of our fellow Texan, Lyndon Johnson.

Guns, Butter, and Buffalo Chips

Robert McNamara was the secretary of defense when Johnson succeeded Kennedy. McNamara had abolished the old "cost plus" system of contract awards and replaced it with "fixed cost" contracts that gave industry an incentive to hold costs down by boosting productivity. Johnson retained McNamara in his post.

But, in October 1964, McNamara issued new orders which gutted the impact of his earlier efforts. He instructed Pentagon analysts to use historical costing as the basis for budget estimates—including an extrapolated cost based on inflation. This destroyed all incentive for military contractors to improve productivity.

In America, productivity in weaponry production has become irrelevant. The most recent example of this is the new Stealth bomber. And, instead of quality control, the military keeps twice the number of weaponry items on hand as are actually needed to fulfill the quota of "full strength." The Pentagon assumes that about half of this inventory will quickly break down in combat.

The debacle of the 1980 raid on Iran to try to free the American hostages proved this assumption correct. It also proved how useless these backup items are in the heat of battle. Several courageous Americans needlessly lost their lives as a result. The world was stunned by our ineptness.

The problems that exist in purely military manufacturing spill over into the manufacture of civilian goods by defense contractors. When, for example, Grumman manufactured city buses, the vehicles proved exorbitantly expensive and quickly broke down. As Texas Instruments became more entwined with the Pentagon, its semiconductor chips failed to keep pace with progress in the industry. They had an unacceptably high defect rate—so high, in fact, that even the military temporarily refused to accept them. Habits of mind formed in the realm of defense contracting, where the sky's the limit on production costs, carry over into the manufacture of civilian goods.

The Johnson administration was the last one in the New Deal tradition of trying to have both "guns" and "butter." Since then, we've seen a parting of the ways. The liberals have taken the "butter," the welfare state—although these days it's margarine, at best. That's the Democratic Party's platform every four years now. The conservatives have taken the "guns," the warfare state. That's the Republican Party's platform every four years now. However, the tragedy involving the Marines in Lebanon, and the near-fiasco of the Grenada action, show that—more and more—our firepower is perceived as merely that of "popguns."

Whichever party wins, whichever platform triumphs, the American people and the American economy lose. The only real difference between the two is that the liberal welfare approach became a failure obvious to all. The only way, God forbid, the conservative warfare approach will be as obvious a failure is if we finally do go into World War III and lose, assuming someone is left alive to note our military failure. That's a big reason why the Republicans keep winning the White House.

Back in the days of New York City's Tammany Hall, political hacks delivered baskets of food and coal to the needy. In return, they got the poor folks' votes, and those of their dependents and other relatives.

Today the practice has shifted to helping entire local economies. The benefactors are politicians in Washington. Calling the baskets of goodies "defense" spending, and covering them with the American flag, does not disguise the fact that the only difference between New York then and Washington now is one of scale, not substance.

Successive administrations, Republican and Democratic, have used these "goodies" to buy votes. In 1978, for example, Jimmy Carter wanted to "goose" the American economy to ensure his re-election as president in 1980. He initiated what was openly called the "Economic Stimulus Program"—in which the Department of Defense got a blank check for military procurement. Carter also wanted to ensure the loyalty of the Democratic "machines" in the big cities for his forthcoming campaign. So he released $440 million in "Urban Development Assistance" grants.

Ronald Reagan vanquished Carter—in part by promising to balance the federal budget during his first term. Carter had promised to do the same thing during his first term, which also proved to be his last. So had Nixon. But neither political party can afford to balance the budget, because the budget can be balanced only by severely cutting back on the buying of votes. And the buying of votes is the real purpose of most of today's federal government expenditures.

Surely no one in the Pentagon seriously believes in the "home port strategy." But the money flowing into Texas to construct a base for the U.S.S. *Wisconsin* helped strengthen the Republicans' position in Texas prior to the 1988 election. As has been repeatedly observed, if the Democrats don't carry Texas, they apparently won't win the presidency.

The Democrats play the same game, as the examples from the Carter administration show. And Texans need no examples from the Johnson administration.

There's an aphorism that says, "You're either part of the problem or you're part of the solution." Texas has always been a big part of the problem, especially when it comes to federal expenditures on the military. Now that our energy and agribusiness industries are in disarray, Texas is particularly vulnerable to the temptation of becoming a welfare state and living on the dole from Washington.

Hence, despite the budget crunch in the state treasury, the state legislature appropriated $25 million at the drop of a brass hat in the Pentagon in order to lure the battleship *Wisconsin* and her escort ships to naval bases to be built on the Texas coast.

Battleships did not even play a significant role in World War II. Yet there was much rejoicing when Corpus Christi won the competition for the *Wisconsin*. The federal government is now firing a broadside of hundreds of millions of dollars into that city. And after the construction is completed, at least $50 million a year will flow into the economy just to serve the needs of the ships and their on-shore support systems.

However, as mentioned in chapter two, the federal government can be capricious. Galveston had also won a piece of the action. Some of the escort ships were to be based there. Galveston promised to spend a lot of its own money on the project, and honored its commitment. But after the election—surprise!—Galveston was suddenly left high and dry. As for the ships: now you see them, now you don't.

Even though the Texas legislature appropriated $25 million for an aged battlewagon, it decided that Texas could afford only one million dollars for the Advanced Robotics Research Institute in Fort Worth. The legislature thus made clear where our official priority remains: the fast buck; federal dollars, not mental capital; money, not wealth; buying into a "get rich quick" scheme instead of investing in ourselves.

Guns are the real bread and butter of Texas. This makes a mockery of all the lip service we give to the ideals of capitalism, competition, and free enterprise.

At least 200,000 active-duty military personnel and civilian employees serve at military installations in Texas. Retired personnel around the state also add their pensions and other benefits to the Texas economy. All told, a good guess is that more than $10 billion a year flows to the Lone Star State through the hands of these people.

San Antonio is the largest city most clearly dependent on the military, in part because its Pentagon funding goes mostly to salient installations such as the Army's "Fort Sam" (Houston) and the four Air Force bases there. Corpus Christi is a close second, with its Army Depot, Naval Air Station, and, soon, the *Wisconsin*. San Angelo counts on Goodfellow Air Force Base; Del Rio, on Laughlin AFB; Lubbock, on Reese AFB. The second chapter of this book noted how important Dyess is to Abilene. The list goes on as to Air Force facilities alone, in cities throughout Texas.

The Red River Army Depot provides the lifeblood for Texarkana's economy, with 6500 Texans making their living by assembling and repairing weapons. El Paso depends on Fort Bliss, and Killeen would cease to exist without Fort Hood. In Amarillo, the Pantex plant has the well-known distinction of being the only place in America where nuclear weapons are assembled (at least legally).

However, the activities which are direct parts of the military are just the start of the total war-related economy of Texas. San Antonio, for example, also gets millions of dollars from "hush hush" Pentagon contracts that go to the Southwest Research Institute there. Austin's only Fortune 500 company is Tracor, a major Pentagon supplier.

Surprisingly, one of the areas most heavily dependent on military contracts is none other than Dallas-Fort Worth, which prides itself on its supposed economic diversity. The "Metroplex" is the major center of military contracting in Texas. The last major recession in Dallas-Fort Worth (prior to the oil woes) was in 1969-70, following a significant cutback in military contracts.

LTV's Vought Corporation subsidiary, along with General Dynamics, E-Systems, Textron's Bell Helicopter division, and Texas Instruments all are heavily dependent on military contracts. General Dynamics, for example, recently had $7 billion in military orders in progress; TI, roughly $5 billion. Mostek failed as a civilian enterprise and has now made its way to the public trough, despite being acquired by a French conglomerate, Thomson. Mostek has been reborn as a war contractor, sharing in a $4.3 billion communications project that Thomson has with GTE for the Army.

In fact, Dallas-Fort Worth is probably even more dependent on the Pentagon than Houston is on the energy industry.

It's difficult to know for sure just how many procurement dollars flow into the Texas economy, because many out-of-state prime contractors use Texas subcontractors, and vice-versa. A ballpark figure, though, is $23 billion—which makes war contracting very big in Texas. Thus the combined total of salaries, pensions, and materiel contracts is $33 billion, which almost makes war the #1 industry in Texas. Yet the usual economic statistics obscure this fact. They categorize procurement contracts within each of the various industries as foodstuffs, manufacturing, and services.

Texas has long provided such meager welfare benefits for individuals that it has ranked near the bottom of all fifty states. Anyone can quickly find an appreciative audience here by declaiming against "welfare chiselers." Whether such attitudes are right or wrong is irrelevant to this discussion. They are an article of faith in Texas.

The supreme irony, though, is that many of our most prominent citizens in government, industry, and labor continue to hustle to win new orders for their local defense contractors, despite the fact that repeated scandals have shown that the biggest "welfare chiselers" of all are the "warfare welfare" recipients in the defense industry. Those who favor defense procurement contracts so highly might recall the original connotation of the term "procurer."

This "welfare state" approach is part and parcel of the Keynesian economics that have controlled the modern capitalist world (other than Japan) for more than fifty years. Whether as social welfare (liberal) or "warfare welfare" (conservative), the American economy has become dependent on the distribution of money by the bureaucracies in Washington. And, as mentioned, Washington, in turn, has become dependent on foreign governments as the source of the money it spends.

The idea that military production is done by "private enterprise" is a hypocritical piety. Any student of business or law knows that what counts is not who holds legal title to assets, but who controls them. Now that the Defense Department controls the activities of roughly 40,000 prime contractors and well over 100,000 subcontractors, it's apparent that socialism needn't take the form it does in, say, Britain. For some strange reason, though, conservatives view this process through red-, white- and blue-colored spectacles, and cheer.

Calling aerospace and other war production "high tech," then praising the high value-added these manufacturing activities bring into an economy, is to miss the point. It again mistakes labels and statistical data for real wealth. Certainly there's a lot of value-added in these industries, and a lot of mental capital. But this value and this capital are virtually sterile.

Granted, all of this military-related activity pumps money into an economy. But that's all it does. It does not help an economy to build up its real wealth, nor to be able to stand on its own two feet without clinging to Uncle Sam's coattails. These industries aren't truly competitive. They do nothing to help America improve its standard of living. And they do nothing to help us reverse the de-industrialization of our basic industries and our civilian economy—which, as the Russian example shows, is also the basis of military preparedness.

It's an open question whether or not traditional welfare payments destroy the initiative of their stereotypical recipients. But there is no room for doubt that "warfare welfare" can destroy the initiative of an entire economy. We have only to look at Virginia, once the leading state of the South, which now has declined to the level of economic "junky," dependent on a brass syringe in the Pentagon for another injection into its economic bloodstream. And Texas is rapidly descending to Virginia's level.

The Return of Opportunity Cost

Regardless of the obvious need for some defense spending, such spending should be regarded as a necessary "evil"—in economic terms—and should be held to the minimum. The minimum, of course, is quite large. And even though this spending is undesirable in economic terms, it is necessary—and in moral terms, praiseworthy.

However, we need to separate the economic harm from the moral good.

There are three reasons why military spending is counterproductive in economic terms. All three involve the opportunity cost inherent in such budgets.

First, neither the organizations nor the hardware created for the military is a real economic good. The battleship *Wisconsin* cannot be used to directly produce new wealth. It isn't a capital good, as an electric-arc furnace or a hydroelectric dam is. Nor can it be directly consumed to provide a higher standard of living in the way that food or medical services are consumed. (There are exceptions: The National Guard is a military organization, but its most important uses to date have been in civilian disaster relief and in riot control.)

Second, the military budget diverts real wealth that's been created in the civilian marketplace. The wealth is appropriated through taxes or through federal debt issues that sop up available funds.

It's bad enough when the government uses the printing press to commandeer resources by outbidding its rivals in the private sector. But when it takes hard-earned cash away from those who need to be creating real wealth, this leaves them with reduced means for doing so. It also raises the cost of capital for the private sector, by forcing interest rates up. All this, in turn, means there will be less wealth available to the government in the future. And this means the government will have to rely even more on debt issues, currency inflation, and (eventually) higher tax rates.

Third, and most important, is the opportunity cost of mental capital. Today, most American engineering graduates find jobs with aerospace and defense contractors (the two are interchangeable). Japan now graduates as many engineers as the United States, despite having only about half the population we do. What's even more critical is that Japan's engineers work on civilian goods and basic industries such as steel. They strive to boost both the productivity and the quality of Japan's manufactures.

In its October 10, 1982 issue, the authoritative industry journal, *Electronics*, reported:

> The nation's electronics industries do not have the technological skills and experience to meet military requirements and at the same time cope with competition from corporations in West Europe and Japan—allies all—in the burgeoning consumer, computer, telecommunications, and test equipment markets ... [Most] of the recent and important advances in electronic technology during the past decade have come despite the Department of Defense and the federal agencies, not because of them. Indeed, the military services are steadily falling behind in their ability to field systems with state-of-the-art electronics, notably computers ... Is there a relationship between the historical dependence of the U.S. electronics industries on weapons markets and their relative loss of world market share in the private sector?

The editors of *Electronics* implicitly answered their own question.

Even when the truly civilian high-tech firms are making progress, they can still suffer as a result of our unthinking support for "defense."

In January 1985, Bell Laboratories announced it had created a one-million-bit microchip, four times more powerful than anything in existence, either in America or Japan. To further develop the chip's potential, Bell Labs needed the most advanced computer available. This was a supercomputer manufactured by Cray Research Company of Minneapolis, the X-MP. Cray made only thirty per year. Bell Labs placed an order.

Then General Dynamics said that it too needed an X-MP for research on the F-16 fighter plane. Cray took the order and told General Dynamics where it stood on the waiting list. But General Dynamics refused to wait. Its people went to the Pentagon and got officials there to invoke a Korean War-era law that allows the military to preempt civilian needs. In the name of national security, the military ordered Cray to deliver its next X-MP to General Dynamics.

Dr. William O. Baker is the retired chairman of the board at Bell Laboratories and a member of the president's Intelligence Advisory Board. "We would feel that the design of a four megabit chip [the next obvious generation of chips] is as vital as any matter that confronts the country at the moment," he said. "It's hard to think of any national security issue that transcends it."

Baker added that the Pentagon has a "fragile and confused priority process. Its allocation of resources to the military is very unskilled and very naive."

One could question whether there was really such a pressing threat of imminent Russian air superiority that would make it so urgent for General Dynamics to delay the Bell Labs program. But what makes this story truly sickening is that, after General Dynamics got its hands on the X-MP supercomputer, it publicly admitted that it really didn't have a need for it after all; certainly, not a pressing need. Apparently the executives at General Dynamics just wanted to throw their weight around and humble the mighty AT&T by showing who's really the top gun in corporate America.

Bell Labs had to wait only a few months for delivery of its X-MP. However, in the high-speed world of high tech, a few months is a long time. One computer executive, who refused to be identified, commented:

> If you have the latest fighter plane, you can protect our shores, but down the road, state-of-the-art technology is the key to our economic security. There's no question that we're in a race for our lives, technologically speaking.

The anonymous executive was referring, of course, to the race against the Japanese.

Earlier in this chapter, we noted Japan's re-militarization. This process has a second aspect, one that's undeniably ominous.

It's a safe bet that the Japanese will manufacture weapons of higher quality and at lower cost than anything the United States can produce. Then the Japanese, being Japanese, will try to export those weapons. This will enable them to improve their balance-of-trade position even more. It also will enable them to ride the experience curve down at a faster rate.

As a result, not only will the United States lose the financial benefit from arms exports, but we will find our national security reduced because other countries will no longer be dependent on us for weapons, spare parts, and other warfare items. This will leave us little leverage for bargaining with countries such as Saudi Arabia.

The example of hostility between a military contractor (General Dynamics) and a competitive civilian firm (Bell Labs of AT&T) may be just the most blatant example of a widespread pattern.

During the drive to raise funds for the Microelectronics and Computer Technology Center in Austin, Dallas leaders pledged they would come up with $5.8 million toward the statewide goal of $23.5 million. According to what at the time was named the *Dallas/Fort Worth Business Journal,* the effort stalled because of opposition from E-Systems and Texas Instruments. Both of these firms are headquartered in the Dallas area. The report said their objections were based on regional jealousy.

Perhaps the deeper truth, though, is that E-Systems and TI,

being military contractors, saw nothing to gain for themselves if the civilian high-technology industry in Texas becomes more competitive as the result of resources generated by MCC research.

The "Lessons of History"

Most Texans have a knee-jerk reaction in favor of anything connected with the military, however counterproductive it turns out to be in practice. Instead of thinking emotionally about defense spending, we need to start thinking rationally about national security—and to persuade the federal government to do likewise.

However, since any criticism of defense spending is immediately labelled as criticism of "a strong America," it's time to discuss the problem in strictly military terms.

The biggest problem America faces in talking about the defense budget is that the question has been polarized along party lines. Liberals, who generally seem to favor appeasement of the Soviet Union, automatically favor a reduction in the defense budget. Conservatives, who generally favor open wariness toward the Soviet Union, automatically favor an increase in the defense budget. Both groups look only at the quantity of dollars involved, not at the quality of national security those dollars are buying.

An example from Texas history is appropriate here, for it avoids the emotional posturing inevitably created by discussing modern defense policy and budgets.

From the very beginning, Hispanic—and later, Anglo—settlers in Texas were subjected to horrid depredations by the Comanches. These marauders also victimized other Indians, and even drove some tribes from the state. During the Civil War, when most white males were serving in the Confederate Army out-of-state, the Comanches struck in a series of devastating raids and forced the frontier boundary back 100 miles.

These were the most formidable opponents that immigrants had to face anywhere in the history of the settlement of the New World. The reason was that the Comanches had both Spanish mustangs and easily reloaded bows. Using rapid-fire techniques while riding full speed on horseback, the Comanches were more than a match for anything the new arrivals could put against them.

Until the arrival of the Texas Rangers, that is. The Rangers' original function was to act as a posse, to track down the hit-and-run Comanches who would otherwise make good their escape.

The formal military apparatus had been completely unable to cope with the situation. The Rangers, in contrast, matched the simplicity of the Indians. In place of the large, slow horses that most settlers used (in part because the horses did double duty by pulling loads and plows most of the time), the Rangers acquired mustangs. Instead of the rapid-fire bow and arrow, the Rangers had the rapid-fire Colt 45 and, later, repeating rifles.

The elaborate network of forts the U.S. Army constructed after the Civil War had proved useless against Comanche raids. Comanches didn't attack the forts; they went after isolated settlers and isolated communities in surprise attacks. Until the 1850s, the U.S. Army didn't even have a cavalry! The Rangers proved to be the only effective defense. And, eventually, search-and-destroy missions proved to be the only effective offense.

At the risk of offending those who measure defense in terms of dollars, there are modern analogues to the Texas frontier situation. For example, Exocet-type missiles have obvious implications for naval warfare. Just one of those missiles sank the British destroyer H.M.S. *Ardshield* in the Falklands war. A similar missile from an Iraqi fighter nearly sank the U.S.S. *Stark* in 1988 in the Persian Gulf. (A second missile penetrated the ship but did not explode. If it had, the *Stark* would have perished.) Exocet missiles cost a mere $250,000 apiece.

Shore-to-ship missiles, such as the (mainland) Chinese Silkworm, were first employed by the Egyptians against the Israelis nearly twenty years ago, when they sank the destroyer *Eilat* in the Mediterranean.

In the Persian Gulf, in 1988, Iranian mines nearly brought shipping to a halt. The United States Navy has invested a billion dollars in each of its carriers—and that's just to build them, not to staff them. The "carrier groups" that escort the flattops cost a total of $20 billion. Yet for all the firepower the American Navy had sent to the Persian Gulf, our forces were nearly helpless against the Iranian mining operation.

The reason is that, in the entire U.S. Navy, there were only two minesweepers. Neither of them was anywhere near the Persian Gulf, because our naval leaders never considered the possibility that the Iranians might use mines instead of fighter planes and torpedo boats as their means of attack.

Minesweepers are relatively cheap. And they're certainly effective. But they aren't glamorous, and command of a minesweeper doesn't exactly put the captain in the fast lane to flag rank. So both the Navy and the politicians, for different reasons, completely neglected this aspect of warfare. The Russians haven't. One of their major strengths is in mining and anti-mining operations. While our Navy prepares to fight World War Three as though it were a rerun of World War Two, the Russians are preparing to fight World War Three as though it would really be World War Three.

Of course, it could be that the people on our side are conducting a disinformation campaign of their own, targeted against the Russians. But a look at recent novels with war scenarios, written by senior military people or with considerable input from them, suggests the West really does look at any possible World War Three as a mere imitation of World War Two. (See, for example, *The Third World War*, by General Sir John Hackett, Ret., and other top former NATO officials; or Tom Clancy's *Red Storm Rising*. A somewhat more realistic approach is Marc Stiegler's novel, *David's Sling*.)

Basically, the Russian naval strategy depends on submarine warfare as well as mining warfare. The Soviet Union even may have developed troop-carrying submarines, to use in commando attacks for securing invasion beachheads.

The Russian navy is not organized around aircraft carriers. It does have helicopter carriers—again, of great value in commando attacks to secure invasion beachheads or to capture vital installations inland. But it only has three carriers for fixed-wing aircraft, and these are not centerpieces of their naval forces.

The Russian army's strategy, on the other hand, is based on the use of tactical nuclear weapons which are fully integrated into the conventional-warfare units. The Soviet Union also is clearly planning to use chemical-biological warfare. Its troops are equipped to defend themselves against CBW and its armored personnel carriers are sealed to keep airborne agents out. The

Russians also have a large capability in offensive CBW, and tested it extensively in Afghanistan.

Those who most loudly proclaim our need for a strong defense against the Russians, and for a big defense budget, have been strangely fixated on a defense policy that assumes World War Three would be very much like World War Two. If they were really concerned about a strong defense, they might also be concerned about the possibility that in the past forty-five years the nature of warfare has changed.

The French were very proud of their mounted knights; the lowly English longbowmen wiped them out at Crecy in 1346. The French didn't learn the lesson, so they were wiped out again at Agincourt in 1415.

Poland was terribly proud of its cavalry—in 1939. The German Panzer tanks cut them to pieces. In 1940 the French were quite proud of their Maginot Line, which the Germans simply outflanked. The Spanish were proud of their armada in 1588. And now we Americans are enthralled with our aircraft carriers.

Those who are truly concerned about national security, and not just using the rhetoric of "America as #1" to camouflage their own ulterior motives, need to take a hard look—not at the defense budget itself, but at the national defense assumptions and conclusions that determine what's in that budget, both in terms of hardware and its cost.

This is where Paul Kennedy's book, *The Rise and Fall of the Great Powers*, is such a disappointment. For one thing, he confines his discussion to the "modern" world (from 1500 on), which is his area of expertise as an historian. But he implies that all the important lessons to be learned about his subject can be learned from studying just those 500 years.

Worse, he insinuates that any given nation enjoys a relatively brief period of supremacy, followed by an inevitable eclipse. In this, Kennedy resorts to historical determinism and thus puts himself in the same category as the mystics. He also sounds like the old domino player in White Oak, Texas, quoted in chapter 2: "We've had our day in the sun. Now we're going to suffer, and there's nothing we can do about it."

Kennedy is correct that at some point defense costs subvert an economy's potential to provide for its own future defense.

However, his book downplays the examples of countries that spent beyond their means for war and severely strained both their economies and their social fabrics—but in the end they triumphed, and the sacrifice was worth it.

He completely refuses to consider that if a determined enemy intent on conquest exists, then a nation has no choice but to spend heavily on defense.

After all, tomorrow is another day. Perhaps the enemy will not be so menacing by then. But as long as a clear and present danger exists, a nation must be ready for war.

The problem in America today is that the particular elements of our defense budget are not serving the interest of national security. They are serving the interest of partisan politics: the pork barrel.

Kennedy's book joins the fray on the side of the liberals who want to cut the defense budget in favor of pork-barrel projects of their own. He does not discuss, at all, the very real threat of world hegemony—even now—by the Soviet Union. Those who deny this threat might consult Edward Jay Epstein's book, *Deception*, and especially Sun Tzu's *The Art of War*.

Kennedy was once an assistant to B.H. Liddell Hart, the renowned military analyst who stressed innovative weaponry, tactics, and strategy. Yet Kennedy does not discuss the changes in the nature of warfare. His former boss would be shocked.

Kennedy's analysis is correct as far as it goes, but it doesn't go anywhere near far enough, despite 540 pages with a wealth of detail. Perhaps the reason why he stopped so short of an adequate discussion of the problem is that he would have had to consider the possibility of Russian aggression. That is no longer a fashionable topic of discussion among respectable academicians.

A Better Role for Texas

If we Texans are to be seriously concerned about America's national security, we must do two things.

First, we in Texas must keep Washington at arm's length, rather than falling into the arms of the Pentagon. We need to extricate ourselves from dependence on Uncle Sam. Only then can we, as a nation, achieve real wealth, economic strength, and the resilience required to be able to deal simultaneously with the commercial threat from Japan and the military threat from the Soviet Union.

Second, we in Texas must work to end the federal budget deficit. This means we must call attention to the need for fiscal self-discipline on the part of the special-interest groups, both in Texas and in the rest of the country, that benefit most from federal largesse. This in turn means that we must practice what we preach and set an example.

Our situation in America has gone beyond the moral issue of cheating future generations of their rightful inheritance. We are already on a downward spiral in our standard of living and our power as a nation. The federal budget deficit drives up the cost of capital, and removes capital from the financial market that would otherwise go to the private sector. Before long, the biggest single item in the federal budget will be the interest payment on previously borrowed money.

As happened to the Southern farmers in their reliance on credit from the furnishing merchants, the percentage of the federal budget devoted to paying interest on our national debt will continue to increase. Our dependence on foreign creditors also will continue to increase—with all that implies for freedom of operation in our diplomatic, military, and economic policies.

Mancur Olson's research, presented in his book *The Rise and Decline of Nations: Economic Growth, Stagflation, and Social Rigidities*, was discussed in the chapter on "Industrial Policy vs. Bootstrap Economics." Olson found that no society or economy in history has succeeded in saving itself from the vicious circle he described. Instead, the pattern has been for an economy to completely collapse, or for a nation to suffer foreign conquest—after which the victor wipes the slate clean and the process begins all over again.

This does not mean that America's doom is necessarily at hand. The only way our economy will revive, however, is through the creation of real wealth. Only by producing civilian goods of a high enough quality and a low enough price to compete with foreign goods, will we ever be able to get the funds to pay off the national debt. We must pay off, or at least enormously reduce, the national debt. We won't be able to do that as long as Washington keeps sopping up huge sums and then pumping them back into the economy in the form of economically sterile expenditures.

We must also insist that our armaments manufacturers improve their quality control and productivity. However, if our politicians continue to use defense-procurement contracts—and defense installations—as a way of buying votes, our genuine national security will continue to deteriorate.

For the sake of keeping themselves in power, our politicians of both parties have been serving short-run special interests instead of the long-run national interest. They have been doing this at our insistence, because each of us is the beneficiary of the spoils gained by one or more special-interest groups. In short, *we* are eating the seed corn of America's future. The politicians are merely handing it out to us, knowing we'll fire them if they stop being such "exemplary public servants."

The Texas economy has always been fragile, but this has become obvious only in recent years. Now, more than ever, we must have strength of character, for only that will enable us to rebuild an economy that is strong, both in Texas and in America. The first step in the direction of building strength of character is to stop making deals with politicians whereby they get our votes in return for "funny money."

We have turned our economy into a house of cards. Each administration, Democratic or Republican, and each Congress, adds one or two cards to this unstable fabrication. Our house of cards still stands, but someday it will fall. And our way of life may well fall with it.

The problem really isn't the federal government, nor is it the professional politicians. The problem is us. As in the children's fairy tale, we are killing the goose that provides the golden eggs. What we do with those golden eggs—such as social welfare or defense spending—is open to debate. What is no longer debatable is that we have all but destroyed our national character, and we are destroying our economy and our national power.

We Americans constantly proclaim that our country is the leader of the Free World. And so it is. But this leadership is only a recent development. As late as the early years of World War Two, we preferred to let other nations take the lead. Usually they failed to do so, and in two world wars America came to their rescue.

Today, there is no nation on earth that will be in a position to rescue us if we fail to exercise our leadership wisely. Hence we must recognize the naïveté of those who say we should take the declarations of our potential antagonists at face value.

There are those who say we should no longer try to exercise leadership. However, whether for or against America's leadership, we tend to miss the most crucial point of all: We are the single most important nation in the Free World. To those who envy us, that fact is more meaningful than whether or not we choose to exercise leadership. As long as we remain the most important nation in the Free World, we still have the potential to exercise leadership.

Therefore, it's not enough for our rivals to try to convince us that we should not exercise leadership. They must work to ensure that we are no longer able to exercise leadership, whether we want to or not. Once our power has declined and other nations have gained ascendancy over us, we will no longer be in a position to effectively look out for our own interests, whether diplomatic, military, or economic.

Wishful thinking about the goodness of humanity has never secured peace for the world. Wishful thinking about the future of our economy is counterproductive to our future security. We Texans have been among the most wishful thinkers of all. We must change now.

13 | Texas: A State of Mind

> *Its prototypic hero is the cowboy: an uneducated, boorish, Victorian migrant agricultural worker.*
>
> —Trevanian
> *Shibumi*

All societies, regardless of complexity, have what might be called a "social ecology." In nature, ecology refers to the way in which various elements in the "ecosystem" are interlinked in mutually enhancing processes. The same thing exists in human society. The economy itself has many interlocking sub-systems, as the chapter on "Growth vs. Development" showed. The economy as a whole is just one part of the larger social ecology.

No matter how strong Texas may be in some areas, it is ultimately only as strong as the weakest link in the social-ecology chain. For a long time now, the weakest link in that chain has been the Texas education system, especially at the primary and secondary levels.

Education, at all levels, has become an important item of national debate in recent years. This chapter will not review the contents of that debate: topics such as the teacher shortage, the lack of pay for good teachers, the continuing employment of inferior teachers, the high school drop-out rate, or the quality of higher education. Instead, this chapter presents a different approach to the subject.

"Bootstrap economics" is a long-term proposal, not a quick fix. It stresses investing in ourselves, mental capital, and value-added. Business-retention-and-expansion surveys and Texas Marketplace programs can do a lot for our economy in the long term. However, we must also examine education, not as some isolated phenomenon but as a vital element of our economic future.

In doing so, we must look closely at the conventional wisdom. The conventional wisdom in economics has proven itself virtually irrelevant at best, and pernicious, at worst. It's quite possible that the same is true regarding education.

For example, many Texans complain about the high dropout rate from our high schools. However, Japan's dropout rate is almost the same. Both Japan and Texas graduate no more than 70 percent of their students from high school. West Germany, another "economic miracle" nation, graduates less than 20 percent its students from the equivalent of high school.

Although this chapter focuses mainly on basic public education through high school, it's worth noting briefly the hue and cry about access to higher education in America and the need for more college graduates. Japan has achieved its stunning economic performance despite the fact that less than 15 percent of its population is college-educated. In America, the figure is more than twice that.

Schooling, in and of itself, does not produce economic development beyond a certain point. In fact, it is quite possible that America reached a "diminishing returns" situation a long time ago. The education establishment still insists that our society is best-served by more people with more degrees, or at least by more people with high school diplomas. However, the evidence is to the contrary.

Instead of looking at the quantity of schooling people receive, we need to look at the quality. We need to build up our genuine mental capital. That is the subject of this chapter.

The Texas Education Reforms

The starting place for a discussion of education in Texas is the Select Committee on Public Education (SCOPE). House Bill 72, which resulted from the committee's work, was passed in 1984. The reforms produced what is perhaps the most important piece of legislation in our state since the Texas Railroad Commission straightened out the mess in the oil industry in the 1930s.

H. Ross Perot, the moving force behind the Select Committee's creation, work, and results, said early on that it was "increasingly clear that the problem started at the top with the State Board of Education." Perot quickly encountered the deadwood and dead minds of a huge education bureaucracy—which shamefully but not really surprisingly included many teachers as well as state government bureaucrats.

The SCOPE reforms were a long-overdue change for the Texas public school system. It was a tremendous act of vision and political courage for the elected officials who backed House Bill 72. Governor (at the time) Mark White, Lieutenant Governor Bill Hobby, House Speaker Gib Lewis, and Comptroller Bob Bullock, among others, joined to provide a great service for the future of the people of Texas. These politicians rose to the level of statesmanship.

The pay raises for teachers that accompanied the education reforms were but a small step in the direction of according qualified teachers the financial respect they are due, in place of the mere lip-service we've always given them. Unfortunately, while the teachers welcomed the pay raise, they thwarted efforts to ensure that only competent teachers remained on the public payroll.

The legislature had enacted a first round of competency tests for teachers. This consisted of general examinations of basic abilities that all teachers should have in common. Many of those who took the exams found them an insult to their intelligence. They should have, because the threshold of competency was set so low that any college freshman should have been able to pass it. Instead, many teachers failed it. Some failed more than once, and were forced out of the schools.

Ironically, our statesmen were then forced to bow to the clout of the teachers' lobby. A second round of competency tests was intended. These would have tested skills of teachers in the specific subject areas in which the teachers were educating students. However, many teachers either lacked confidence in their own abilities or else knew outright that they lacked such abilities. They convinced the teachers' lobby to try to sabotage the second round of (specialist) competency tests. And the lobby succeeded, by persuading the legislature not to finance the second round.

The result is that while students must now pass competency tests to graduate from high school, they may well be taught by incompetent teachers who were "grandfathered in" to our public school system.

Even so, it wasn't just the teachers and the education bureaucrats who subverted some of the intended reforms. SCOPE also had sought to have the State Board of Education become a non-partisan appointive body. This would have been a potentially significant improvement over the traditionally elective nature of the Board, whose members run as Democrats or Republicans.

The issue was decided by a referendum. Urban voters approved the change. Those in the suburbs endorsed it by an even wider margin. However, the rural voters overwhelmingly condemned it. They also turned out in sufficient numbers to offset the results in the other areas.

Apparently the rural folks used the School Board referendum to register their opposition to the "no pass, no play" rule. This rule had curtailed the extracurricular sports activities of high school athletes whose academic performances were unsatisfactory. Football is dear to the hearts of Texans. For some, it's dearer than the future of our children or our economy.

The rural argument is that many students have no aptitude for the life of the mind, but are quite good athletes. Therefore, such students should be allowed—even encouraged—to downgrade the life of the mind in favor of developing their physical skills.

However, the life of the mind isn't something reserved only for scholars, nor even for those who are highly intelligent. Anyone familiar with "higher education" knows there are a lot of people in academia who are inclined toward intellectual subjects, but who don't have much intelligence, let alone intellectual ability.

The life of the mind, at the bare minimum, means the ability to think clearly. Surely this is something that's just as valuable for future athletes as it is for future Ph.D.s, future managers, future factory workers, and all other future adults, regardless of how they earn their living. The odds against even the best high school athlete's ever becoming a professional athlete—and especially the odds against that person having a long career—are overwhelming. Even the very few who will succeed in professional sports will find that being able to think clearly will keep them from being at the mercy of their agents, lawyers, and managers.

Those who created the "no pass, no play" rule were doing all high school athletes a favor. Those who opposed the "no pass, no play" rule were, in effect, betraying their own children's future in order to further their own desire for cheap thrills on Friday nights at high school football games.

Still, there are valid grounds for at least some criticism of the SCOPE reforms. The "back to basics" movement, of which House Bill 72 was a part, is vital to this state's future. However, while it was absolutely necessary, it was not in itself sufficient. Students need to be able to read well, to do numbers, and to be able to recall important facts from memory. However, all of this provides tools, just as language itself is but a tool. These tools provide forms through which we can express our thoughts, and facts on which to base our thoughts. But they do not by themselves ensure that the content of those thoughts is worthwhile.

Not all of SCOPE's changes were positive. Some might have a negative effect. According to Jon Brumley, then-chairman of the State Board of Education, "The schools will teach to the tests." He explained that the school curriculum in Texas, and teachers' activities, will revolve around the questions on the competency tests.

He also pointed out that the actual score required for passing the tests was even lower than the official score. This is because the initial scoring did not grade the questions students were most likely to answer incorrectly. As the competency test program takes hold in our schools, he continued, the answers to those more difficult questions will be included in the scoring. Eventually, still more difficult questions will be added—in physics, chemistry, and mathematics.

If Brumley's forecast represents the on-going practices of the Texas Education Agency, then teachers are superfluous. Teaching machines could do this work just as well, probably better, and at a fraction of the cost. Ironically, this strategy strengthens the case of the teachers against competency testing for themselves: If the teachers in our schools are merely to help students memorize answers to forthcoming tests, then there's no need for the teachers to be competent in those subject areas after all.

The back-to-basics movement is supposed to emphasize basic skills. That's good. However, it now mistakes the skill of memorization for the three R's. What started out as a good thing has become too much of a good thing. By simply doing more of the same, the back-to-basics movement is becoming counterproductive.

Those who teach children (versus those who teach adults) must be able to respond to the child as a complete human being, instead of relating only to a highly specialized area within the pupil's mind. Teaching, properly understood, is much like psychotherapy. The teacher has to be able to work with each child in a subtle and interactive manner. He or she must find the right pedagogic approach for each child as an individual. The teacher ought to find out what makes each child "tick." Then the teacher can present subject matter to each child in such a way that all will have the best chance of getting the most out of the education experience.

If we instead treat our schools as factories, where teachers are assembly-line workers who attach components to work-in-process that moves along an academic conveyor belt, then we have destroyed the meaning of the life of the mind. The word "education" comes from a Latin term that means "to lead out of" or "to bring out of," not "to stuff into."

Real education is not something that ends with the conclusion of formal schooling. Nor is it something that only starts when students leave high school and enter college. The formal education, instead, provides the basic resources that will enable us to continue to educate ourselves, informally, for the rest of our lives.

The new State Board of Education needs to take the next step in upgrading our schools' programs. This involves teaching students how to think clearly. The competency tests, while necessary, are product-oriented. They test mastery of vocabulary and math, for the most part, as well as rote memorization of an array of facts.

Thinking, on the other hand, is process-oriented. And the most important factor in learning how to think is mastery of simple logic.

Experts will always know more facts than laypeople will. Further, experts will always try to exclude laypeople from decision-making because laypeople "don't know all the facts."

However, no expert, no matter how well-informed or brilliant, can defy the simple rules of basic logic. Logic is far more than common sense. It is the ability to take an argument apart and see if it fits together in a convincing manner.

The Media and the Message
For example, a lot of people are upset by the alleged bias of the media. Television, especially, presents dramatic images that provoke a highly emotional response. That is the nature of the medium, so those images are unavoidable. Since our emotions operate at a deeper and more powerful level than our intelligence, these images can prove decisive in shaping public opinion. In the hands of reporters and news directors who are grinding a political axe, this is dangerous.

The only way to overcome this power is by making sure that people can think clearly. Then, after the images are gone from the screen, the power of a logical argument can help people overcome the knee-jerk reactions that would otherwise result from the dramatic, emotional images on television.

Our age is dominated by non-written communications. In a sense, then, knowing how to think clearly is more important than knowing how to read, write, or do numbers. Fortunately, these basic, simpler functions can be taught to children at the elementary school level. Therefore, it's not a matter of sacrificing these skills in favor of logic.

However, our entire education system is stuck in the literary tradition. Education leaders are constantly filled with surprise, anger, sadness, and resentment toward students who obviously dislike school.

Most students intuitively understand that our education methodologies are obsolete. For some time now the world has been in the electronic age. Yet school systems are still devoted to a bizarre hybrid of 18th-century horse-and-buggy and 19th-century factory approaches. Those who get ahead in our academic system and who eventually assume positions of power in that system are those who can function well within our outmoded schools. They quite naturally assume that the approach that brought them to success is the right approach, and they support continuation of the status quo.

This is ridiculous. For those who would dispute this charge, consider: Our current approach to education is almost as irrelevant as was the requirement that all college students master Latin and Greek and then study materials written only in Latin and Greek. Anyone today who suggested a return to the classics as the basis for all education today would be laughed off the campus. This is because academia finally acknowledged—but not until the turn of the last century—that the classics were not the alpha and omega of education.

Those who insist that reading and writing continue as the be-all and end-all of contemporary education need reminding of the furor that occurred when writing was first introduced as a pedagogic method 2500 years ago. None other than Plato and Socrates—heroes of the "back to basics" movement—thoroughly denounced written study materials. They said that reading and writing subverted the students' ability to truly learn.

Don Sneed is an associate professor of journalism at San Diego University, and a former member of the Texas A&M faculty. He has put the case for making students "media literate." In his words:

> In this, the Information Age, students need to learn about and use the variety of media they are constantly exposed to and through which they gain much of their understanding of the world. Because information plays such an important part in our lives, students should be introduced to the wide world of visual, graphic and verbal communications in addition to receiving instruction on the literary classics and essay-writing.
>
> This proposal is not intended to replace English-as-we-know-it or learning to write. Instead, the presence of media studies in a curriculum would signal that writing mastery is but one of the skills that people living in the 21st century will need as new informational technology emerges.
>
> What media studies would do best is to have students make connections between their culture and their schoolwork while they develop reading, writing, speaking, listening and—most importantly—critical thinking skills. After all, huge numbers of students are turned off by the literary classics and writing essays but are

turned on by the movies, video cameras, tape recorders, radio, popular music, magazines, television soap operas, videocassette recorders, and even comic books and newspapers . . .

Students should be taught how to become confident media consumers and users. They should know something about advertising, public relations, propaganda and news . . .

And yet no hue or cry is heard to bring media studies into the curriculum. Perhaps the reason is that such a notion sounds almost like it might be fun, and, for goodness sakes, something fun can't also be educational.

Perhaps Sneed has put his finger on the crux of the problem. Generations have come to think of school as drudgery, maybe even as a prison in which adults place students. If each of us will but reflect for a moment on our own schooling, we must acknowledge that what occurred in the classroom was usually the least pleasing aspect of our educational experience. Yet, so caught up are we in this that we assume this is the way it should be, as though primary and secondary education ought to be a children's version of "boot camp" for the life of the mind.

The United Negro College Fund uses the slogan, "A mind is a terrible thing to waste." How true. How many minds are we wasting because we have arbitrarily maintained a slavish devotion to outworn tradition?

Sneed goes too far by implying that, just because comic books and television soap operas "turn on" a lot of students, therefore they should be studied in school. Despite his zealotry, his essential points are valid.

The first of these is stated openly, that learning ought to be an enjoyable experience. The second is implicit. Sneed hints at, but does not discuss, the value of "media literacy" in helping us cope with the intended manipulation of our minds by "advertising, public relations, propaganda and news." Students who are adept at using the tools of modern telecommunications will also be able to recognize the alternatives that are available in the presentation of any message. This awareness should further enhance their ability to know when the creators of any given message have deliberately presented it in such a way as to attempt to manipulate the receivers of that message.

Sneed does not say that media studies should displace reading and writing from the curriculum. The diehards who denounce media studies seem to believe that the mere ability to read and write somehow guarantees that people will, as adults, read only good books, newspapers, and magazines.

However, a quick look at the publications that comprise the vast majority of the general public's reading material ought to make the diehards wonder if their dogmatism is justified. But no. Rather, they look at the trash that provides the fare of most of the electronic media, and retreat in horror to the alleged purity of the written word. They refuse to acknowledge that if our schools had truly educated students, there would not be the huge market for all the trash—including the printed trash.

Instead of dealing with the world as it is, the diehards simply exhort people to read more good books. Their self-righteous aloofness only plays into the hands of those whose commercial—and political—interests reside in discouraging the general public's ability to recognize quality at all, whether printed or not.

Aristotle noted that the greatest danger facing democracy was the ease with which it can degenerate into mob rule. We still think of "mobs" as gatherings of people in one place, such as a lynch mob or a riot. But it's apparent that manipulative electronic media can turn us into a different sort of mob. In this new mob, each member is physically isolated from the others in his or her own home. Yet each responds as part of the "group think" of a mob that's been created by media imagery.

And, as so often happens, we mistake form for content. Where there is no crowd, we assume there can be no mob. However, the essence of a mob is that its members do not think clearly and are easily manipulated. The literary purists conveniently forget how "yellow journalism" in the heyday of the newspapers sometimes turned the entire United States into an atomized mob.

Problem-solving with regard to math questions or finding the best word with which to complete a sentence does not in itself make for education. Artificial-intelligence machines can do these things quite well. This isn't the life of the mind, because there's no human element, or at least no fully human element in the sense of the humanities. By denying the human element's potential for good, in the way that the competency tests do now, we almost make inevitable the human element's potential for evil—as in the case of electronically induced mob rule.

The future now envisioned for the competency tests points up the distinction that Richard Hofstadter (borrowing from Max Weber) made between genuine intellectuals and what he called "intellectual journeymen": The former lives *for* ideas, the latter lives *off* them.

This isn't just an idealistic distinction concerning humanitarian values. It has vitally practical implications. To return again to Burton Klein:

> Asserting that formal education plays an important role in determining the rate of progress in no way explains how progress comes about. To explain how progress comes about one must start with a description of the actual process involved in pioneering new technologies.

Klein's book, *Dynamic Economics*, does just that. In it, he also noted this:

> Only by possessing imaginative entrepreneurs, who can generate new ideological mutations, can societies hope to evolve in the face of new circumstances.

The key word is "imaginative." And this brings us to one of the most amazing ironies of the "back to basics" movement.

Critics of America's education system point to Japan's economic success. They also point to Japan's education system. They then assume there is a cause-and-effect relationship between the two. Had these critics mastered basic logic, they would have realized that this argument, as presented, is sheer nonsense: "False cause" is the logician's term.

Even though Japan has scored some devastating successes vis-a-vis American business, most observers pin their hopes on entrepreneurship and on corporate "intra-preneurship." They say that the Japanese are good at copying, and at improving what they copy, but the Japanese are not so good when it comes to fundamental creativity. Whether this is true or not remains to be seen.

But, if it is true, then what sense does it make to turn the American education system into a copy of Japan's—and thus destroy the imaginativeness and creativity that are our main hope for future economic successes?

Some critics of America's education methods point to the deliberate effort in Japan's schools to eliminate competition among students in the classroom, and say America should do likewise. These critics fail to add that Japan's education techniques are geared entirely to rote memorization. Further, the benign environment of the classroom quickly gives way to a devastatingly harsh, and final, system of exams that only test students' ability to memorize. Japan's education system is an extreme example of competency testing. Those who fail to make top grades often commit suicide. Their deaths give Japan the highest juvenile suicide rate in the world.

Asking the "Right" Questions

Most people are acquainted with the bilateral symmetry of the human brain. Simply put, the "left brain" is the locus of rationality, logic, and analysis. The "right brain" is the site of creativity, synthesis, and intuition. The problem with competency tests is that they are strictly left-brain oriented. And, at that, they are inadequate because they omit logic. They cannot possibly test for imaginative thinking, nor for creativity.

Nor can they test for true intellectual ability. We confuse intelligence and intellect in our education. In part this is because first-rate intellectuals also have first-rate intelligence. However, there have been many people of genius, but who have not been intellectual. Lyndon Johnson, a political genius, was not at all intellectual. Bobby Fisher, the former world chess champion, is brilliant but no intellectual. Henry Luce, founder of the Time-Life empire, was another genius who was not at all intellectual.

If we convert our education system in Texas to a test-oriented curriculum, then our graduates will merely be human robots. They will not have the mental aptitudes of real human beings, insofar as creativity and imagination are concerned. If Klein's argument is correct, what we will need most in the future is the ability to ask the right *questions*, not the ability to come up with the one "right" answer to a question that's simplistic and narrow in the way that it defines a problem.

This brings us back to the problem of "risk internalization," first discussed in chapter 9. If we are to develop the ability of our students to reason, they must be encouraged to search for new questions—for which even the teacher doesn't have the answers. This is a form of risk internalization, because there is no longer a final certainty. Neither students nor teachers can take it easy, knowing that there is a "right" answer that will conclude their search for knowledge.

"Right" questions are those that prove most helpful in organizing the search for new knowledge and in providing the best inputs to reason about. Education becomes a never-ending process, which is what it should be.

This has two implications. First, apparently our education establishment doesn't know how to educate students this way. Nearly all research into teaching methods is intended to produce maximum efficiency in boosting students' test scores. Second, learning how to ask the right questions implies that the students can question the teacher's questions, and the teacher's answers.

To encourage risk internalization among our students, we must also encourage it among our teachers. This isn't something that results from cramming for a competency exam, nor even from reading a textbook or a teacher's manual. It results, ultimately, from high esteem. Only high self-esteem will give our teachers the self-confidence to handle students' questioning of the conventional wisdom—including the conventional wisdom espoused by the teacher.

Risk internalization also implies trial and error. It can't occur when the so-called trial and error consists merely of trying to find the one right answer—which the teacher already knows. Risk internalization is possible only when all the participants realize beforehand that they never will find the one right ultimate answer ... at least, not if the question is worthwhile.

The Relationship Between Process and Product

This is not to say that education should become a series of "bull sessions" devoid of reference to a body of subject matter that students should have mastered. If students are going to be taught how to reason, they must have something worthwhile to reason about. And to be worth serious thought, that "something"—or series of "somethings"—must be fairly sophisticated. This implies that the subject matter be inherently profound, such as different interpretations of historical events and the lessons to be gained from them.

If the students don't know anything about the events to start with, then they can't reason about them. So the traditional approach of mastery of facts goes hand-in-hand with the development of clear thinking. However, our system has traditionally stressed the former to the virtual exclusion of the latter.

Nowhere is this more obvious than in the study of science. The "back to basics" people decry our students' ignorance of and disinterest in science. So the reformers want to require students to study more science. However, the reformers have completely forgotten that we've been through this before.

The most recent previous stress on science followed the Russian launch of the world's first satellite, Sputnik, in October 1957. Just as people today speak of how we're falling behind the Japanese, back then people said we'd obviously fallen behind the Russians.

Suddenly tens of millions of dollars came from the federal government to outfit physics and chemistry labs in high schools and to train more science teachers. Schools beefed up their science requirements for graduation. "Science fairs" popped up in school districts throughout the land.

More than thirty years later, what do we have to show for it? All those students who were supposed to "turn on" to science and major in the sciences in college and become professional scientists . . . never turned on.

The number of science degrees granted each year has steadily declined. Foreigners comprise 50 percent of the graduate student body in the sciences, and make up an alarming proportion of the professional scientists in this country. Even more alarming, as "underdeveloped" countries have become developed, many of these foreigners are going home. America faces a desperate shortage across the board in the sciences: teachers, professors, researchers—and students who are American and thus will probably stay here to pursue their careers in science, and in technology.

What has happened is not what was supposed to happen. Yet no one asks where we went wrong. Instead, the "back to basics" people want to require more students to study the sciences, as though this will preclude our future shortage of devoted professionals. If it didn't work before, why would it work now? Especially considering that the ability of students to read and write and do numbers (all vital to science) is demonstrably worse now than it was then.

It's apparently never occurred to the new reformers that the real problem is the way we *teach* science (and everything else, for that matter). More than in any other discipline, the pedagogical methodology in the sciences consists of nothing but rote memorization and "experimentation" that repels all but those who already love the sciences.

We do nothing to help students become aware of the wonder of science, per se. Instead, we mouth platitudes about "the scientific method," and then pretend that having students dissect a frog in a biology lab will somehow make them appreciate science in action. We teach the history of science—any science—in a way that sweeps under the carpet all the fierce struggles among competing theories, the breathtaking discoveries that caused people to understand themselves and their world in completely new ways. The intimate connections between science and philosophy and the arts and even politics are ignored.

Most important of all, by failing to inculcate a genuine understanding of the scientific method, we ensure that students will never realize that science is the most exciting combination of fact and theory that is humanly possible, because scientists can use the facts to test theory in a way that no other human endeavor can.

And then we are so surprised when the post-Sputnik generations turn, en masse, to astrology, the occult, and "scientology." The proliferation of such nonsense is itself proof that something is terribly wrong with the way we teach science in our schools. Yet we are surprised when so few students choose real science as a career.

We didn't solve our science problem after Sputnik by throwing money at the teaching of science and requiring students to study science. As Giorgio de Santillana, the historian of science, said: "Those who will not learn from history are doomed to repeat it."

The Employee's New Role

Another problem with our 19th-century attitude toward education is that the future role of students is implicitly based on the military model. This distinguishes between officers and enlisted personnel. The economic "officers" (corporate managers and professionals) will give orders, and the economic "enlisted personnel" (laborers and clerks) will obey the orders—without having to understand why. That model worked well enough in the late 19th century, but it is obsolete today. Yet even now our schools apparently assume that understanding "the reason why" is something to be reserved only for college students—the future "officers."

The creation of "Quality Control circles" has already begun to demonstrate the need for change, but only in a small way. Employees can contribute more if they understand the reasoning behind the production process and the nature of the product or service they're working on. So the employer benefits from having workers who can think clearly.

More important, in a way, the employee benefits from being able to think clearly, and not just in terms of rewards to be gained in his or her present job. As David Birch commented in *Job Creation in America:*

> In today's world security must flow from the individual, not the job. Few jobs are secure; the only security derives from the ability to adapt and move, and these derive from the strength of the individual. By strength is meant the possession of a scarce resource in any period: general knowledge that can be quickly adapted to new circumstances. It is the ability to perform several jobs and to concentrate on one or another when the need arises—and to understand the principles involved rather than memorizing the manual that describes how something is done.

Times have changed, and the nature of the employee's role in business has changed, even in the "blue collar" and "pink collar" jobs. These changes will work their way through the economy. As robotics, cybernetics, and artificial intelligence take over the roles of mechanical human thinking and physical labor, it's all the more important to make sure that human beings enhance their creative and critical intelligence.

The ability to read and to express oneself clearly both in writing and orally are still very important, and will remain so. Even though employees can't rely on "memorizing the manual that describes how something is done," they better be able to read it, understand it, and quickly look up what they need in it. However, while all this is still necessary, it is no longer sufficient.

In order to, in Birch's words, "understand the principles involved," students (future employees) must be able to question the questions and the answers. This is especially important at the level of junior and senior high school. Partly this is because students are closer to adulthood here, and ought to be able to handle more difficult mental tasks. More important, though, it's because most students will not go on to college. These years are the last chance the education system has to help these students learn to think clearly. (This ability should prove even more beneficial to those who do go on to college.)

Unfortunately, it's at the junior and senior high school levels that society, and many teachers, feel that it's most important to force students into a mental straitjacket and to not allow any challenges to authority.

Authority, discipline, and rules are vital. Encouraging students to make intellectual challenges to the conventional wisdom does not mean that students should be permitted to disregard authority, discipline, and rules.

But if democracy is to survive, we must understand that intellectual freedom is every bit as important as economic, political, and religious freedom. If fact, they are inseparable, one from the other: Everything that's now called economic, political, or religious was at one time only an idea in one person's mind.

Because most students will not be continuing their formal education beyond high school, it's especially important that they gain a healthy respect for intellectual freedom—and for the self-discipline that makes freedom different from license and anarchy. There's no point in trying to get students to think clearly if, from the very beginning, their thoughts are subjected to censorship.

Spoon-feeding "pat" answers to simple-minded "thought questions" may enable students to improve their grades on tests that include essay questions. However, it won't help them (or us) cope successfully with the intellectual free-for-all of the world's cultural, political, economic, and religious debates.

The Porpoise of the Blue Dolphin

A case in point concerns a young Texan named Scott Ward. At the time in question (1986), he was all of ten years old. Another fellow named Scott, whose last name is O'Dell, had written a novel called *Island of the Blue Dolphin*. The book was first published in 1960, and had quickly won the Newbery Medal for the most distinguished contribution to American children's literature. *Island of the Blue Dolphin* is assigned reading in many U.S. schools. Since its first publication, it's had more than 7,000,000 readers.

Scott Ward was a fifth-grader at Boone Elementary School in Alief, Texas. He noticed something seemed wrong in Scott O'Dell's math. As he explained in a letter to the author: "On page 60, Karana killed three dogs. On page 76, she killed two more. I thought she had killed a total of five dogs. When I read page 92, the book said she had killed four dogs. Is this an error?"

What makes this highly significant as an illustration of the education system is the response Scott Ward got when he brought the discrepancy to the attention of his teacher. His letter continued: "My teacher said a Newbery book would not have an error in it and I was wrong."

Ward's fifth-grade teacher may have been having a bad day, and the response may not have been typical. However, as Ward's letter also mentioned, when he persisted in his enquiry, "My teacher would not answer me and said I was wasting class time. I decided to ask you." Hence Scott Ward's letter to Scott O'Dell.

O'Dell, his book's original editor and proofreader, and millions of schoolchildren and teachers had, for a quarter of a century, missed an obvious error that it took a ten-year-old in Alief, Texas, to catch. And while his discovery in itself was hardly earth-shaking, the attitude he encountered at school is grounds for a shake-up.

Fortunately, O'Dell was not only still alive, he was far more receptive than Scott Ward's teacher had been. He admitted the error, and commended the boy. But it was only because of that child's courage, self-confidence, and ability to think clearly that the problem was resolved.

How many other potential discoveries, far more important, have been thwarted by narrow-minded authoritarian attitudes toward educating our children?

This example also demonstrates the difference between mastering the basics and going beyond them. It also demonstrates the need to do both. If Scott Ward couldn't read, or couldn't read well, this situation would never have occurred. Likewise, had he been unable to add three plus two and come up with the correct answer of five. His obvious ability to think clearly would have been of much less value if he had not already learned how to read and to add. Having mastered the basics, he was prepared to go on to some critical thinking of his own, however modest its scale.

It's quite correct for our schools to give all children certain basic mental tools in common, and to show them how to use those tools;—i.e., how to think clearly. But having done that, our schools must not dictate what the students shall think. Rather, our schools must encourage students to learn to think things through for themselves. Then they must provide a forum in which all students who so desire can bring their various insights to bear on a given subject and find their own understanding enriched by the insights of others.

The Practical Payoff

Again, this isn't "just" some notion of humanitarian idealism. Its implications are as practical as they are vital to our future. To again turn to Burton Klein:
1. Firms are likely to generate impressive advances only as long as they employ a wide diversity of people who engage in a good deal of conflict as to how to achieve certain generally accepted goals.
2. Firms are likely to remain internally interactive and able to deal with a high degree of uncertainty only as long as they are prodded by their competitors.

Klein's book makes clear that his discussion of "conflict" does not refer to office intrigue, nor to internal warfare. Instead, he's referring to the competition of ideas. If students, and businesspeople, have the courage of their convictions, and the openness to be receptive to the insights contained in other people's convictions, then any given subject or problem will get its most thorough discussion. We will all profit from this, whether in terms of economics, culture, politics, science, or religion.

This is the essence of progress in any sphere of activity. Romantic idealists praise democracy's respect for individual rights as a good thing in itself, but they often let their appreciation go at that. Pessimists denounce democracy's insistence on protecting minority rights, and on hearing out all sides of a question, because this impedes swift action. However, democracy is a way of bringing together people with widely diverse ideas. These ideas compete in the political marketplace and policies are shaped as a result.

In other words, democracy is the best way known of dealing with political uncertainty, just as capitalism is the best way known for dealing with economic uncertainty. Both involve a high degree of risk internalization and competition, receptivity to negative feedback, openness to hints from the environment, the serendipity factor—and, above all, acceptance of predictable unpredictability.

By respecting individual freedom, which includes the freedom to challenge the group (or the teacher, or the boss, or city hall), we can provide the best means of enabling a group to adapt and to survive the challenges of uncertainty. The interactive process is vital.

The Need for Self-Reliance

In her book, *For Your Own Good*, Swiss psychotherapist Alice Miller wrote that each one of us must find his or her own method of self-assertiveness. This self-assertiveness is the psychological analog to mere physical survival. Without it, we waste away as human beings. In her view, we become obedient puppets whom others manipulate.

Self-assertiveness is really just the outward form of an inward feeling of self-respect. Self-assertiveness, as the example of Scott Ward shows, is precisely the trait our schools seem most determined to stifle. And if competency tests dominate the educational process, then they will mentally cripple the very students whom the acquisition of basic skills is supposed to help. Not only will pupils become "obedient puppets" manipulated by the schools, the schools themselves—and the teachers—will become obedient puppets manipulated by the government.

Only a psychological slave allows others to walk all over him or her. Yet our schools seem to insist that all children should always been meek, kind, and "good." Miller however, says that to demand this and simultaneously expect children to be authentic and honest is absurd. She goes on to say that this places an impossible demand on children which can cause more conscientious and sensitive children severe psychological conflict and disruption.

It is conscientious and sensitive children and adults who are most aware of what's happening in their world. (Again, the example of Scott Ward is apropos.) For the sake of entrepreneurship—not to mention other reasons, even more important—we need more people who are attuned to the changing social ecology, and who can ask themselves and others intelligent questions as to what's going on, and why, and what can be done about it.

This is the function of criticism, which is a form of aggressiveness (or preferably, "self-assertiveness"). If we do not allow our students to learn how to responsibly criticize their environment, including their educational environment and their teachers, then their aggressiveness will be channelled destructively.

Drugs, for example, are a form of destructive behavior; in this case, self-destructive. Those who are so upset about the increasing use of drugs and of alcoholism among young people need look no further than the schools those young people attend. There, even before the education reforms, students were "reduced to the instrument of another person's will." Yet at least drug and alcohol abuse are "only" self-destructive. In many other parts of the country, the alternative form of destructiveness has been chosen: juvenile delinquency, especially in the form of highly lethal gang warfare.

A recent study at Duke University's Medical Center lends credence to this line of thought. Dr. John Lochman headed the research effort there, which tested a new explanation for juvenile abuse of drugs and alcohol: a lack of ability to constructively express natural aggressiveness. Lochman ran a program of "anger coping" for boys in elementary school. Here is a wire service account of the project and its results:

> Boys who were aggressive in elementary school but were taught to cope with anger showed significantly less alcohol and drug abuse three years later than untrained aggressive boys.... Their drug use was only a quarter of that reported by untrained boys, and measures of marijuana and alcohol use generally ran about half of those for untrained boys...
>
> The treated boys showed improved self-esteem, which may have removed one reason for using drugs, Lochman said. They also had improved problem-solving skills, which may have prepared them to make more careful, less impulsive decisions about using drugs and alcohol, he said.

The findings of the study should be regarded only as preliminary, not conclusive. Still, as one medical observer commented, "It's a very, very promising piece of research." Students who are considering drug use have already rejected adults as valid authority figures. To reach these young people, it is pointless for an adult to tell them "Just say 'No!'"

The very command to "Just say 'No!'" is itself an arbitrary, authoritarian one—and may well exacerbate the very behavior it hopes to eliminate. Facile injunctions such as these demonstrate a complete lack of understanding of the psychological problems faced by potential drug users. Perhaps they also demonstrate a disguised unwillingness to allow children to become authentic and honest adults who are *not* obedient puppets whom others manipulate. The demand that students "Just say 'No!'" clearly arises from an attitude that young people are—or ought to be—obedient puppets to be manipulated.

The ultimate purpose of helping people learn to think clearly for themselves is that they will develop some wisdom. Wisdom isn't something that springs, fully developed, from the brow of individuals. It's usually the result of trial and error. Michael Maccoby, in his business book *The Gamesman* (which was an enormous best-seller some years ago), commented:

> People think of qualities of the heart as opposite to those of the head. They think heart means softness, feeling, and generosity, while head means tough-minded, realistic, thought. But this contrast is itself symptomatic of a schizoid culture, in which the head is detached from the rest of the body ... The head alone cannot give emotional and spiritual weight to knowledge in terms of its human values. The head can be smart but not wise ... Unlike the head, the heart is not neutral about knowledge ... Thus the heart is the seat of consciousness, in contrast to conceptualization, which is in the head ...

> The opposite of doubt is not certainty, but rather faith in our experience and the willingness to risk being wrong, and, worse, gullible. It is easier to take this risk if we know that with effort we can think/experience ourselves back to the truth. In contrast, certainty implies control and predictability. For both the detached intellectual and the hard-headed fanatic, it is the facsimile of conviction.

It all fits together: mental capital, value added, investing in ourselves, risk internalization, receptivity to negative feedback, openness to hints from the environment, predictable unpredictability, the serendipity factor. All of these, in turn, are—or ought to be—part of our educational system as well as of our economy.

In the past, we have used the school system as just a training ground for future employees. A good school system should still have that role. However, it should never have only that role. Instead, both education and the source of one's livelihood as an adult are, in America, meant to enhance the quality of each individual's life. Thus, instead of making school subservient to the needs of the workplace, we need to recognize that school and work are just two points on the same continuum, two facets of our existence. But both are ways in which we can make our lives more meaningful and enjoyable.

Life, Liberty, and the Pursuit of Happiness
This book has made much of entrepreneurship. In recent years, it's become fashionable to extoll the virtues of the entrepreneur.

Insofar as this is a much needed corrective for the previous years of worshipping the "organization man," and then the years of condemning all businesspeople, it's good.

But most entrepreneurs fail. The usual reason given is that they suffer from under-capitalization. Yet deeper examination offers much evidence that under-capitalization is just the effect, not the cause, of a failure of mental capital.

A lot of people become entrepreneurs for the wrong reasons. These people are doomed at the outset. It seems that the most important knowledge an entrepreneur can have is not so much the knowledge of the product or service he or she is selling, and not even the knowledge of the market and the competition, but knowledge of himself or herself. And this is what "right-brain" skills, or "the heart," can provide. The "left brain," the "head," cannot.

Ultimately, this gets each of us into a question of what we want out of life. And this is a question that each of us must answer for himself or herself. Just as too many people go into the arts or music so they can parade about and strike the pose of "artistes" who have supposedly risen above the allegedly crass world around us, so too many people become entrepreneurs in the false hope that commercial success will bring them great happiness. Deep inside, they know this is not possible all by itself; and so, often, they accidently-on-purpose set themselves up for inevitable failure. The pattern is really just a vastly more subtle version of those who turn to drugs or alcohol as their chosen path to salvation—with the difference that drugs and alcohol, if abused, are a guaranteed path to oblivion.

Getting in touch with ourselves, and being able to articulate our feelings and thoughts, has an importance beyond its relevance to each of us as individuals. As public issues have become more complicated, less clear-cut, we have relied too much on labels as a substitute for understanding. Words such as "hardliner" and "liberal," especially, have been used as a way to describe someone with just one term, and to thus avoid more serious in-depth analysis. Not only is this practice sheer laziness, it's also dangerous.

The very idea of democracy is based on gaining input from a wide variety of people—in fact, from everyone who will be affected by the outcome of a policy discussion and who wishes to contribute to that discussion. The core concept is one of reasoning, together. If we instead choose to give one (flattering) label to ourselves, and a different (derogatory) label to those who don't immediately and completely agree with us, then we have set in motion a process whereby persuasion inevitably degenerates into force. If public policy-making is dominated by an "us" vs. "them" mentality, and we deny at the outset that those who disagree with us just might be right, even in some small way, or that we just might be wrong, even in some small way, then dialogue becomes a travesty.

Freedom is not something that can exist within just one area of a society and not others. The habits of mind, and of behavior, that freedom entails are such that they cannot be restricted to one activity. Totalitarian nations understand this quite well. We in America do not. But we in America also do not seem to appreciate that freedom is not really an end in itself. It is a means to an end, to social progress, increased happiness, and more meaningful lives for us all. If we don't know how to use our freedom in a responsible way, then we will eventually reject freedom as the means to attain the ends we seek.

Freedom means competition, and it means criticism. Children who aren't allowed to understand the meaning and value of freedom and criticism become adults who still don't understand them—and who thus might deny their exercise to others.

For the sake of our political future, as well as our economic future, we must build up our mental capital in all areas of society. The only way to do that is through the competition of ideas. Texas ought to truly become a state of mind.

14 | Starting Over

Sentimentalism ... asserts that the values a society's activity denies are precisely the ones it cherishes ...
—Ann Douglas
The Feminization of American Culture

In the ancient Greek myth of Sisyphus, that poor fellow was condemned by the gods for eternity. His punishment was to roll a boulder up a hill. When he reached the top, the boulder would roll away, down the hill again. Sisyphus then had to retrieve it and start over.

We Texans are in a similar situation. For awhile, we fancied that we were "king of the hill." But now our good fortune has slipped from our grasp.

We've been through something like this twice before. The first time was during the Yankee "Reconstruction"; the second, during the "Great" Depression. However, in neither of those cases had Texas made it to the top of the heap before disaster struck.

Another difference between our situation and that of Sisyphus is that he was the victim of intervention by the gods. We aren't. We did this to ourselves—with a little help from Arabian petro-politics, among other things.

But this means that we can attain our freedom, regain mastery over our economic future. Thus, we can keep this from happening again.

This book started off by noting that a lot of economic cures recommended for Texas are touted as "instant remedies." Unfortunately, as Americans, we are especially prone to the search for the quick fix. We're always looking for the magic wand to wave over our problems to immediately correct everything.

The alleged solution to our problems is always something very simple and very easy to do, more or less. This is part of our "one factor" approach: There's only one cause of our problems, and we need use only one means of dealing with it.

We like to keep things simple. There's nothing wrong with that, as long as simplicity is appropriate. But in the real world, things tend to get complicated, and to stay that way. We can't just cut through them the way Alexander the Great lopped off the Gordian Knot.

This book has made a lot of demands on its readers. Unlike most books about public policy or economics, it hasn't discussed the situation in terms of only one factor. Nor has it confined itself to simplistic matters comprehensible only by those of mediocre intelligence.

For seven years now, the Texas economy has gone from bad to worse. Some say that our economy has now turned around. Even though they've been saying that in each of the past seven years, perhaps this time they're finally right.

However, the Texas economy will be vastly different in the future from what it has been. With or without a recovery, we have largely signed our future over to outsiders in a way that we've never done before.

When the major banks in Texas were becoming mere subsidiaries of major banks in other parts of the country, many Texans cheered. They proclaimed that out-of-state banks would be putting a lot of new money into the Texas banks. This in turn meant that a lot of new money would be coming into Texas, it was said, priming the pump for an economic recovery.

It's true that the acquiring banks put a lot of money into the Texas banks they bought—but not in the sense implied by those who trumpeted the sellout. The Texas banks had lost so much money that their capital bases were eroded. The money that got "put into" Texas banks was, for the most part, a mere bookkeeping entry: an addition to the capital account. This does not mean that the acquired banks suddenly got more money to lend.

In fact, it's quite possible that the Texas subsidiaries of out-of-state banks will serve as sump pumps, taking financial liquidity from Texas and putting it into pipelines headed for New York, California, Ohio, and North Carolina.

Earlier, this book mentioned the Texas banker who took all the money in the banks he controlled and put it into blue-chip bonds. The deposits and assets on the books of his banks gave the impression that his banks' money was still in Texas. Not so. The local communities his banks served were left out in the heat, to wither and die.

This is quite likely to happen on a statewide scale now. The out-of-state banks that have acquired Texas banks know their own economies a lot better than they know that of Texas. Executives in distant headquarters will be making the final decisions on what loans are granted, and how much of the banks' total funds will be allocated for loans in Texas. It seems a safe bet that most of the money deposited in "our" banks by Texans will be loaned out to borrowers in other states.

However, the biggest impact will be on small business. It usually costs at least as much to process a small firm's loan application as it does a large firm's. But the profit on the large loan is higher, in part because it's easier to keep track of one large loan than a lot of small ones.

So most of our banks will not be interested in talking with small businesses about loans. Just as oil-related firms now cannot get loans from most banks, so will small firms in almost any industry be left empty-handed.

And if the evidence presented by Birch, Jacobs, Klein, and Olson is correct, this means that we in Texas soon will be "out of the frying pan and into the fire." In short, we ain't seen nuthin' yet. The effects of the capital starvation of small business won't be so dramatic, in the sense of being the stuff of newspaper headlines and features on the evening news. But they will be far more pervasive than the spectacular failure of a large firm, and just as permanent.

We have seen how, in the oil industry, the large firms cut their operations in marginal areas and closed their branch offices. They moved key personnel to Houston and Dallas to "hunker down" and await better days.

If a national recession occurs, a similar pattern will show up in the banking industry. The big banks in New York, California, Ohio, and North Carolina will start taking losses on loans in their home states. They will need more funds to cover their operations.

Because the economy will be in recession, they won't be able to get those funds by issuing securities in the financial markets. Instead, they'll lay off employees in Texas and close offices. The cash flow thus saved will be redirected to their home offices.

Banking is just the most obvious example of what's happened in many industries in Texas. The Texas economy, seen strictly in terms of statistics, may well recover. But the statistics will mask the deeper truth.

More and more well-paid Texans will be mere vassals of out-of-state corporations. And most new jobs in Texas will be low-skill, low-wage jobs in local distributing operations that are mere branches of out-of-state firms. An increase in the employment rolls will not by itself reveal these facts.

Our federal officeholders may gain more influence as the population of Texas increases, but they will answer to the corporate executives in other states who control the banks, the corporations, the jobs, and the cash flow in the local political districts. In short, our leaders will become mere "hollow men" (and women), not solid ones. Their economic masters in other states will not permit the rise of any activities here that will challenge them, either economically or politically.

It may already be too late to make a serious effort in Texas to gain economic independence. But if we don't start soon to make such an effort, we'll be stuck in our rut for a long, long time. Why, Texas might even descend to the level of *Oklahoma*. And if that prospect isn't enough to get Texans concerned, then our situation is truly hopeless!

As David Birch's work indicates, the foundation for our future prosperity is small business: firms with twenty employees or less. These are the companies that can contribute the most to really get Texas moving again. These are also the firms that have the most to gain once the Texas economy does start moving.

Burton Klein's research and analysis show that the conventional wisdom of economic development is flat out wrong. The Oregon Marketplace and the New Jersey business-retention-and-expansion surveys have proven that Jane Jacobs's research and theories are valid, beyond a doubt. We in Texas (and the rest of America, for that matter) need to apply the lesson learned from these people and projects, in the form of "bootstrap economics."

However, "bootstrap economics" is not a quick-fix solution to our problems. It's a long-term program. In place of the high-profile glamour of junkets to New York City or Japan, it is simply a program of getting down to brass tacks inside the state. Instead of looking for overnight miracles, it anticipates a lot of work and a view to the long haul.

The business-retention-and-expansion surveys and the "marketplace" program can make all the difference in the world for the future of Texas—if they're done right.

At times it appears the "Not Invented Here" syndrome is at work in Texas. Even though we say we're willing to learn from others, a misplaced sense of Texas pride sometimes seems to prevail. A few organizations in Texas have devoted fairly substantial resources to learning about economic development efforts elsewhere and implementing them locally. But then they virtually waste their investment by deliberately ignoring the most important "do's and don'ts" of the instruction they received.

It's one thing to change something that's worked elsewhere, to make it better here, once we know, from our own experience, how we can make it work even better here than it has elsewhere. It's something else to change the system around even before trying it out, simply because we want it to be different for the sake of being different: uniquely Texan.

The people in New Jersey and Oregon have been quite willing to share their knowledge with Texans. We shouldn't feel ashamed because we need to borrow from them. As the Japanese have shown, he who plays follow-the-leader today just might *be* the leader tomorrow.

The efforts in New Jersey and Oregon made mistakes, which their people acknowledge. We need to learn from their mistakes, not repeat them. Thanks to their example, we in Texas don't need to start at "square one." But neither should we start by looking for shortcuts to "square six."

Others have accumulated a vast amount of mental capital that's ours for the asking. They have already pushed the experience curve rather far along; we can ride that curve farther, starting out at a point not far behind where they are now. We don't have to re-invent the wheel. In fact, what these other efforts have created is far more advanced than a mere wheel.

However, local economies in Texas shouldn't expect to work ninety-day wonders. No doubt we will run into problems that the folks in New Jersey and Oregon have not yet even encountered. Perhaps some of the solutions to their problems just won't work in Texas, even when the problems appear to be the same.

We need to crawl before we walk, let alone run. While some may impatiently dismiss that suggestion, even crawling is better than lying sprawled on the ground—which is exactly where we've been for several years now.

As the recent histories of hundreds of firms and individuals in Texas have shown, the know-it-all who thinks he's found a way to get richer, faster, than it's ever been done before, is the guy who's headed for a big fall. We in Texas have already taken a big fall. Our local economies can't afford any "get-rich-again-quick" schemes.

We have to put in a lot of years of slow, painstaking efforts, with little immediate payoff. In other words, haste makes waste. And we can't afford to waste anything, anymore.

Ironically, the biggest problem we face is the Texas habit of thinking only on the "grand scale." For the most part, local economic-development organizations are not interested in small-scale efforts. Instead, they only want "big ticket" projects. Yet, by now it should be clear that the cumulative effect of hundreds, perhaps thousands, of small-scale efforts will be greater than that of one massive "showpiece" facility. More importantly, with "bootstrap economics," local communities will no longer be staking their future on just a handful of large, local activities. Further, the state of Texas will not be betting its future on the performance of just a handful of "key" industries.

We simply must stop thinking in grandiose terms and stop looking for a magic wand to wave over the Texas economy. There is no magic wand, not even "bootstrap economics."

Typically, people in small business have all they can do just to take care of their own business—especially now. The large firms have the surplus resources to assist local development efforts. But as this book has shown, such efforts to date have been virtually counterproductive.

It's time for the people with small businesses to make their influence felt in Texas. This does not require a sacrifice of time or money. It does require little things such as writing letters to state legislators, to the state Department of Commerce, and to local economic-development organizations. Too often, it's too easy to decline to do these things, on the grounds that something as insignificant as writing letters won't make a difference.

But, collectively, they can make a difference—a very big difference.

Instead of allowing our future to go, by default, in the direction of more of the same, we need to turn things around. If people in small business won't take even the small measures required to protect their future, then they will have no excuse if their future is one of oblivion. While "bootstrap economics" may not be the solution to all of our problems, it at least gives us a fighting chance. It's a damn sight better than whining, on the one hand, or indulging in escapist fantasies on the other.